The Story of Old
Ste. Genevieve

Other books by the author:

The Old Cathedral, 1965 (2nd edition, 1980)

The Oregon Trail Revisited, 1972 (2nd edition, 1978; 3rd edition, 1983; 4th edition, 1987.)

History of the Hazelwood School District, 1977

Legacy: The Sverdrup Story, 1978 (2nd printing, 1987)

Leif Sverdrup: Engineer Soldier at His Best, 1980 (2nd printing, 1986)

Maps of the Oregon Trail, 1982 (2nd edition, 1983; 3rd edition, 1990)

Challenge: The Sverdrup Story Continues, 1988

Images of The Santa Fe Trail, 1988

Impressions of the Santa Fe Trail: A Contemporary Diary, 1988

Maps of the Santa Fe Trail, 1989

The Santa Fe Trail Revisited, 1989

The Story of Old

Ste. Genevieve

Gregory M. Franzwa

*To my pal,
Jean Tyree Hamilton,
with best wishes
Gregory M. Franzwa
February 28, 1992*

The Patrice Press

Second Edition: January 1973

Third Edition: January 1983

Fourth Edition: October 1987

Fifth Edition: September 1990

**Library of Congress
Cataloging in Publication Data**

Franzwa, Gregory M.
    The Story of Old Ste. Genevieve / Gregory M. Franzwa.
    —5th ed.

        p.   cm.
    Includes bibliographical references and index.
    ISBN 0-935284-86-9 : $5.95
    1. Sainte Genevieve (Mo.)—History.   I. Title.
F474.S33F7   1990
997.8'692—dc20   90-46150
                                                           CIP

Published by
The Patrice Press
1701 South Eighth Street
St. Louis MO 63104
1-800-367-9242

On the cover: Diorama of a street scene in colonial Ste. Genevieve
in The Old Courthouse, St. Louis. Courtesy Jefferson National Expansion Memorial.

Printed in the United States of America

To Ted, Scott, and Chris

Contents

Preface

Ste. Genevieve is a sleeper. It isn't listed in many travel directories; the pocket encyclopedias rarely mention it; it gains only passing note in the national tour guides. Yet, it has more historic integrity than many of the great nationally known historic towns which attract millions of visitors each year. Here one may walk up to the Ribault House and place a hand on the upright posts that form both foundation and wall. These are the same posts that were here two centuries ago. The house has been restored, but it hasn't been reconstructed.

Without taking anything from the dedicated rebuilders of Colonial Williamsburg, it must be acknowledged that such an act cannot be experienced there. Although that presentation is skillful and accurate, much of it was done from the ground up.

Or go into the attic of the Guibourd-Vallé House in Ste. Genevieve. Lay a hand on that old Norman truss, adzed into shape and pegged into position in 1806. It's the same old truss. The same pegs. Right where they were.

Go to Old Sturbridge Village in Massachusetts.

There are fine, honest old houses there, but for the first two hundred years of their existence those buildings might have stood in Ohio.

Ste. Genevieve is a Mississippi River town of about 4,500 people, some sixty-five miles downstream from St. Louis. Largely because of the difficult farming conditions in the area, it was declared a depressed area by the U.S. Department of Labor in 1965. As such it qualified for a study grant from the Economic Development Administration of the U.S. Department of Commerce.

Acting on a request from the Ste. Genevieve Tourist Bureau, the EDA commissioned the St. Louis firm of Allied Engineers and Architects (a joint venture of R. W. Booker and Associates and Hellmuth, Obata, and Kassabaum) to determine what could be done to make the old town a major tourist attraction, thus creating new jobs for the area. A team of outside specialists was retained by AEA to assist their own staff with the study, and this team included the author.

Although I was not totally ignorant of Ste. Genevieve, having visited it in 1959, I must confess that I looked upon it as an old town with an old house in it. During the course of writing my first book, *The Old Cathedral,* which has much to do with the history of the area around St. Louis, I was surprised to note the abundance of history in Ste. Genevieve. But it wasn't until I affiliated with the AEA team in May 1965 that I actually discovered the wealth of structural mementoes from the reign of the Bourbon kings.

I shall never forget my first night in Ste. Genevieve. Shortly after midnight that spring, I left my room in the Ste. Genevieve Hotel and walked alone through those ancient streets. Walking past the old home of

Commandant Jean Baptiste Vallé, I could see the towering hickory Council Tree in the moonlight; on past the darkened Old Brick, which once echoed to the revelry of a bygone era; past the majestic old church; by the silent galleries of the Guibourd House; and on into the old cemetery, where the graves seemed to be bursting with their secrets. The sky over the Mississippi was light grey before I returned to the hotel. The love affair was on. It still is.

Since I am formally educated as a journalist and not a historian, I felt it imperative that a most thorough job of research be undertaken before writing the manuscript of this book, if for no reason other than to keep it from being cut up by the professionals. With the aid of Dr. Felix Snyder, director of libraries of Southeast Missouri State College, Cape Girardeau, a bibliography exceeding sixty titles was assembled. This was augmented by hundreds of newspaper clippings, old pictures, and all manner of data and old books proffered by the people of Ste. Genevieve.

Perhaps it should be mentioned here that for all the history the old town contains, its record is extremely well hidden. Those who have written on it — even the experts — seem to have erred in places. Records were kept only when they were essential to the administration of the church, military or civil law. For example, the archives do not indicate the year a house was built. Rather, they date the earliest recorded transfer of property. Whether the land was improved at that time is not always stated, and whether the improvement was that which is there today is left to the educated guesser. Births, marriages, and deaths were carefully recorded, however.

The field research was both confusing and amusing.

Personal examination of the houses themselves — the structural members, hardware, millwork, and sash — was fascinating. Talks with the owners were equally delightful, and often contradictory with the supposed facts, documented or otherwise. Some owners were careful to point out that their stories were unsubstantiated; others insisted they were true, substantiated or not. The process of sifting and checking was laborious indeed.

One of the most rewarding aspects of my work was my reception in Ste. Genevieve. I was never refused admittance to any of the old homes. The owners stopped whatever they were doing to escort me personally, pointing out the various features with understandable pride. I was lunched, wined, dined, and talked to death. I loved every minute of it.

A lot of others helped me too, and without them there would be no book — people like my former colleague and good friend, Bernard K. Schram, who employed his literary expertise to bail me out of some otherwise embarrassing entrapments, and Frankye Donze, who opened many doors. Vera Okenfuss, a walking encyclopedia of the lore of Ste. Genevieve, Vera-fied the text. Bill Kiefer of the Bank of Bloomsdale was most helpful in many areas.

I am indebted to Leo Basler, who took a day off to escort me to some of the outlying sites; to Joseph Wolf, who missed lunch to escort me to the Saline Spring; to Charles Cassoutt, who opened the sacristy of Kaskaskia's Church of the Immaculate Conception for me; and to the noted steamboat authority, Frederick Way, Jr., of Pittsburgh, who supplied the documentation on the *Dr. Franklin II*. E. J. Schaefer, president of General Pass Book Company, took off the better part of a day for an interview. Ralph W. Smith not only gave me unlimited rights on his excellent tour map but offered to change it any way I felt necessary.

From St. Louis there was the seemingly limitless cooperation from the women comprising the library staff of the Missouri Historical Society, who worked long hours to help me find the facts.

Leonard W. Blake, vice-president of the Missouri Archaeological Society, donated much of his knowledge and the use of his personal library to the cause.

I was most gratified by the gracious manner in which Dr. Ray Breun of the Jefferson National Expansion Historical Association offered the use of the slide reproduced on the front cover.

To the proofreaders I am especially grateful: Anton A. Tibbe, Charles H. Ellaby, Jr., and my patient wife, Laura, — each caught their share of bloopers. My sister, Candace K. Franzwa, put all those little doodads on the French words, bless her.

Anybody out to make a fast buck off any supposed libelous statements will find himself reckoning with Carroll J. Donohue, senior partner in the distinguished law firm of Husch, Eppenberger, Donohue, Elson, and Cornfeld. Donohue looked at the manuscript with an eye toward our fiscal well being.

I am indebted to the good offices of Joseph Weber, vice-president of Stanley Photo Company, for obtaining the use of a new Kalimar Six/Sixty single lens reflex camera, and to George Winslow, vice-president of Kalimar, Inc., who provided it. Weber selected the camera because it has the inherent capability of making an amateur's work look professional. L. Allen Klope gets the credit for the photographic printing —

his superb darkroom was a hotbed of activity for many long nights. Ray Cliff, president of Runder Studios, processed our negatives with great skill and tolerance. My friend and client, Roy N. Sutton, offered the use of a brand new IBM typewriter to prepare the final draft.

My colleague, Donald H. Marshall, volunteered to undertake the public relations work on the book. Dr. Ralph W. Booker, A. G. Hayes, Harry Greensfelder, Jr., and Herbert R. Hellrung — clients all — were most patient with me during the trying days when the manuscript was under way.

Jane Howe Kiel used her great knowledge of the English language on our behalf, unsplitting the infinitives and undangling the participles; and John Kiske, Jr., and William B. Muckler, from the printing company and the typographic house, respectively, did their part with expert applications of their specialized knowledge.

The book, however, would be hollow to me without the advance reading and critical commentary of two towering figures in the scholarly world of architecture and history — Dr. Ernest Allen Connally, chief of the Office of Archaeology and Historic Preservation of the National Park Service; and Dr. John Francis Bannon, S.J., chairman of the Department of History of St. Louis University.

I am deeply grateful to all of them.

Gregory M. Franzwa
March 15, 1967

Preface to the Second Edition

The efforts of Lucille Basler to update the first edition are gratefully acknowledged. Basler, an untiring

worker for the betterment of Ste. Genevieve, has
devoted many hours to our cause, and we thank her for
it.

Shortly after the first edition was published, a
motion picture was made, based upon the book, and
entitled *Ste. Genevieve — A French Legacy.* A production
of KETC, Channel 9, St. Louis, the film went on to
win high honors from the American Association of
State and Local History, and has since been shown in
more than 300 metropolitan areas.

January 1, 1973

Preface to the Fourth Edition

In 1986 our Patrice Press published *Colonial Ste.
Genevieve,* by Carl G. Ekberg, Ph.D. This is the most
advanced study yet of the period and has had the effect
of knocking many of the prior suppositions about old
Ste. Genevieve into a cocked hat. That book has since
won a number of high honors from scholarly organiza-
tions.

In 1987 Osmond Overby, Ph.D., professor of architectural history at the University of Missouri-
Columbia, completed his project to add scientific
method to the dating of some of the most important
houses. I am indebted to him for his early release to me
of his findings.

The work of these two scholars has been incorporated into the fourth edition of this book. Their
authentication of the facts renders the story of this
community even more remarkable.

An additional appendix has been supplied. Lorraine
Stange prepared a research paper on the nicknames of

Ste. Genevieve — a work so enjoyable that we have chosen to share it with our readers. It is presented with our gratitude and respect for its author.

Gregory M. Franzwa
Summer 1987

CHAPTER I.

River on a Rampage

Any resident of any Mississippi River town can testify that Ol' Man River can come boiling out of his banks at any time, even in the middle of a prolonged drought. It's what's up north that counts. A fast chinook over the Yellowstone country can do it, or a balmy April sun over the snowfields around the Falls of St. Anthony.

History doesn't record what kind of a spring it was in Ste. Genevieve. That there was a flood of monumental proportions — possibly the most significant flood in the history of the Mississippi Valley — is attested to by the fact that the date 1785 is known by hundreds of the 4,500 residents of the town of Ste. Genevieve, Missouri, more than 200 years later. *L'anné des grandes eaux* — the year of the great flood.

It is known, however, that the little village strung out along *le grand champ* — the big field — had been subjected to floods with some regularity in years gone by. As early as 1780 the river had undercut the bank to such a degree that great sections were toppling into the current. By 1784 a few of the citizens in some of the oldest houses abandoned them and headed for the high ground upstream or the bluffs to the west. Then, in 1785 it hit.

The angry waters sucked away more sections of the bank, boiled up over the little trail, licked at the cedar stockades surrounding each habitation, and sent each citizen scurrying to the high ground with whatever possessions could be carried and those livestock that could be herded.

One of Auguste Chouteau's keelboat captains, riding his cumbersome vessel down the swollen torrent to New Orleans, maneuvered out over the town in wonderment and tied up at the top of a stone chimney to survey the damage. There wasn't much to survey — a few other chimney tops, the ridge of a hip roof here and there, and water almost as far as the eye could see. The damage seemed to be total.

As the black waters receded, leaving in their filthy wake the decaying remains of entrapped fish, livestock, and plant life, the dejected settlers picked their way through the foot-deep mud to their homes. They came to François Vallé II, many of the 594 citizens, and Vallé, son of their recently deceased commandant, heard their concerns.

If an Indian is seen breaking into the stable to steal the horses, a ball can be put between his eyes. There will probably be another one the next night, but if the habitant is a light sleeper and a good shot, the word will get around soon enough and he'll keep his horses. A ton of shot can be fired into Old Man River and all that will happen is that the water will rise a little farther. The question was resolved — the town had to move, and the people would stick together.

Just as *le grand champ* had been their betrayer, it also had been their friend. A move of any distance would put them out of reach of the enormous fertility of that piece of bottomland which had supported them so well for thirty-five years. After all, it was said that one could leave an adz on the plain overnight and by morning it would have baby adzes.

So the roll was called, and they answered — the aged Baptiste La Rose, said to be the first settler; Don Sylvio Francisco de Cartabona and his troops — the military detachment; J. B. Sebastian Pratte; Louis Bolduc; Vital St. Gemme Beauvais; the merchants Datchurut and Viviat; Jean Baptiste Beauvais — all most likely were there. "Misère," as the light-hearted Frenchmen had nicknamed their sodden little village, was to be abandoned. Those homes or portions of homes that could be salvaged would be moved to the high ground a mile or two upriver, to *les petites côtes* — to the little hills. Those whose losses were total would build anew. And *le grand champ* would continue to feed the village.

This, then, was the culmination of an era which had begun some thirty-five years earlier with a French nobleman, a dozen miners, and twenty-two black slaves; an era which pitted the gentility and culture of Versailles against the engulfing wilderness. Or perhaps it began much earlier — in the mists of the eighth millennium before the first recording of time — about 12,000 years before Christ.

CHAPTER II.

Pre-History of Ste. Genevieve

The slowly changing ways of life of the prehistoric inhabitants of the area have been divided into four basic stages by archaeologists. These generally follow each other, but often overlap. The period of the earliest hunters is called Paleo-Indian, dating from before 10,000 B.C. to around 5000 B.C.; the succeeding stage, Archaic, dates from before 5000 B.C. to after 1000 B.C. in some places. The Woodland period in this area comes from the time 1000 B.C. to about 1300 A.D.; the Mississippian culture is known to have existed from around 900 A.D. to 1500 A.D. and later.

Archaeologists have found little more than stone tools and weapons to indicate the presence of Paleo-Indian groups in Missouri, but the types are similar to those found in the American West at kill sites of big game animals which now are extinct. It may be assumed that clothing was worn, since the climate was cooler and wetter than now. The scattered findings of remains of these people indicate that they probably lived in small nomadic family groups. If the earliest hunters were not at the site of old Ste. Genevieve, the spear points found in the vicinity indicate they certainly were nearby. The Mississippi served as a great magnet. Saline Creek, about six miles south of town on U.S. Highway 61, may not have been there at that early date, but if it were, that salt meant a game lick. Where game was available, the Indian was not far away.

People of the Archaic culture, who were of Mongoloid stock, lived in hunting and gathering groups, and moved around in small bands that briefly joined together when food was abundant. Bone needles indicate the use of sewn clothing to cope with the cold.

Early Woodland people in Ste. Genevieve, identified by the beginnings of pottery making, first became apparent about 1000 B.C. and gradually changed into Middle Woodland a few centuries before Christ. The culture is marked by development of plant cultivation, a more settled life, and more complex burial practices.

Middle Woodland included in many places an elaborate culture, called Hopewell by the archaeologists, which existed for several hundred years.

Although villages were small, large burial mounds containing exotic and artistic offerings were constructed, and differences in the burials indicate a well-developed caste system.

Trade contacts to obtain burial offerings were widespread. These included seashells and alligator teeth from the South, raw copper from the Lake Superior region in the North, mica from the Appalachians in the East, and obsidian, a volcanic glass, from the Rockies in the West.

The Old Fort, a ceremonial enclosure at Van Meter State Park, midway between Kansas City and Columbia, was built by the people of the Hopewell culture.

This Middle Woodland variant went into a rapid decline in the early part of the Christian era, and archaeologists are not agreed as to the causes.

The succeeding Late Woodland period, which lasted in places after 1300 A.D., was much less elaborate. The occupation sites, although usually small, are very numerous throughout Missouri, indicating a population increase. On those sites are found considerable numbers of tiny stone projectile points. Some students of prehistory suspect that this indicates general use of the bow and arrow. These tiny points, popularly called "bird points," on the head of an arrow shaft could kill a deer or a person.

It was the Mississippian culture which left its mark upon Ste. Genevieve, so strongly and indelibly that it remains there today. Believed by some archaeologists to have originated along the Ste. Genevieve-St. Louis axis about 900 A.D., this culture gradually expanded both upstream and downstream, leaving massive earthworks in its wake.

Middle Mississippian cities sometimes contained thousands of people. The women carried out an extensive agricultural economy, growing corn, beans, sunflowers, squash, and gourds. The men were hunters and warriors. The great truncated pyramids often were topped with elaborate temples, and these were surrounded with numerous houses, arranged in accordance with the social prestige of the occupants. Some of the houses were square, some were circular. Early historic accounts indicate that great religious rituals were carried out. The entire town often was protected by a pointed stockade. Implements, although of stone, usually were well made and relatively efficient. The Mississippians, like those of the Hopewell

At 16 feet 1 inch in height, the great Mississippian mound on le grand champ is considerably smaller than its original size. It is along the east side of St. Marys Road, two miles south of South Gabouri Creek.

culture, carried on extensive trading with most areas of the United States, even as far north as Lake Superior, where they found copper. They used dugout canoes, generally hollowed from cottonwood logs, to traverse vast distances on the Mississippi River and its tributaries.

The Mound Builders of the Middle Mississippi culture left their earthen legacies throughout much of Missouri. One of the greatest cities was located at to-day's Cahokia Mounds State Park in East St. Louis, Illinois. Louis Houck, one of Missouri's foremost historians, located some 28,000 mounds in the state, documenting them in his three-volume *History of Missouri* published in 1908. (One archaeologist observed that Houck must have paid his reporters by the mound, since the actual number seems to be less than half that. But that's still a lot of mounds.)

. One of the most spectacular prehistoric earthworks in the state is on *le grand champ* on the St. Marys Road (Highway 61), some two miles south of Gabouri Creek. There are eight definite mounds on this site. The principal one is about 250 feet wide and 300 feet long. Others are considerably smaller and range up to only two or three feet in height. Houck stated that the largest mound at this site was twenty-five feet high. Six years later a writer named Bushnell put it at fifteen feet. The archaeologists Adams, Magre, and Munger must have measured the mound in 1941 (they are too scientifically oriented to have guessed) when they put its height at thirty feet. Measurement with an eye level by the author early in 1967 revealed that the height of the great mound has been reduced to sixteen feet one inch.

Leonard W. Blake, vice-president of the Missouri Archaeological Society, stated that the large mound probably was not a signal mound, as is sometimes reported, but was almost certainly a temple mound. Blake believes the smaller mounds could have been burial mounds. This culture often laid its dead on the surface and piled dirt atop the bodies. Smaller mounds surrounding the large one indicate a religious significance.

The mounds in *le grand champ* are all under cultivation today and probably have been for some 200 years. Before whites arrived they probably felt the plow of the decadent remnants of the Middle Mississippi culture for another 200 years. They currently are being plowed to precipitate leveling. Therefore, it is reasonable to assume that if the big mound is sixteen feet high now it certainly must have been much larger when it was completed.

There have been no excavations at the big Ste. Genevieve mound. Presumably it will be plowed, planted, and plowed again for succeeding generations, until no mound is left at all. Surface collections have been made — literally bushel baskets full of potsherds, flint chips, and stone artifacts have been picked up. Most were of such little value to the finders that they were dumped in the weeds along the Valle Spring branch, where they are today. Substantial shards of great, thirty-inch salt evaporating bowls have been uncovered along the Saline, some of them 600 to 700 years old — relics of the great Mississippian culture which settled there.

Explorer Hernando de Soto, in his midcontinental meanderings in the early 1540s, is believed to have contacted the Middle Mississippians extensively, and consequently contributed to their disintegration as an advanced culture. He brought with him numerous European diseases, for which the Indian had no resistance. He also exercised cruelty toward his hosts, causing entire cities to be abandoned to the conquistadors and breaking the homogeneous cultures into fragments unable to sustain themselves.

By the time the intrepid French penetrated the Mississippi Valley the culture had died out.

CHAPTER III.

Explorations of the Middle Valley

Before proceeding further into this narrative, it should be in order to address some of the claims that seem to have had their origins in the promotional file of a chamber of commerce rather than in a researcher's notebook. One: Coronado did not get to the Mississippi — near Ste. Genevieve, St. Louis, or anywhere else on that river. He didn't even get to Missouri. Contemporary historians cannot in good conscience bring Coronado closer than a point some 200 miles west-southwest of Kansas City. Two: de Soto did not get to the Saline Spring. None of his men did. Again, reputable historic researchers cannot place de Soto much closer than Memphis, some 225 miles downstream from the Saline.

Much of the ruckus about de Soto developed around his procurement of salt, desperately needed as his ranks thinned rapidly for lack of it.

One of the finest accounts of de Soto's expedition was written by Garcilaso de la Vega, the son of an Inca princess who followed Pizarro in Peru. Garcilaso spent much of his life compiling an account of the exploration from firsthand reports of survivors of the adventure. The following account, quoted from the 1957 Varner translation of Garcilaso, took place when de Soto was in Arkansas, somewhat west of Memphis:

> Thus on inquiry he found among his men eight Indians who had been seized on the day the Spaniards entered the town. These people were not natives of this place but strangers and merchants who in their trading passed through many provinces and included salt among the things they customarily brought to sell. When taken before the Governor, they declared that in some mountain ranges forty leagues [about 120 miles] distance, there was a great quantity of very fine salt. And in answer to the repeated questions put to them, they replied that also in that land was much of the yellow metal about which the Spaniards had inquired.
>
> Two soldiers, Hernando de Silvera and Pedro Moreno, were sent on the mission, carrying various articles of barter.
>
> With this accord, they departed, and at the end of an eleven-day journey returned with six loads of crystalline rock salt, which had not been made artificially but was formed naturally, and in addition brought a load of very fine and resplendent brass. They reported however that the lands they had seen were not good, but sterile and poorly populated.

Garcilaso's reports are not accurate throughout, but even if the contingent were camped exactly 120 miles from the Saline this could hardly have been the source of the salt. Scholars of the expedition have established that de Soto crossed the Mississippi south of Memphis. There is no brass around the Saline; however, there is copper in western Arkansas. Surely they would have heard of the great Middle Mississippian city only three or four miles upstream. The salt in the Saline is obtained by evaporating it in bowls — it is not "formed naturally" — and there is hardly any ground on earth more fertile than the Mississippi bottomlands around Ste. Genevieve.

The area was not really opened to Western European civilization until some 130 years after de Soto, with the voyage of Pere Jacques Marquette and Louis Joliet.

While the area was penetrated by the Spaniards, it was left to the French to perform the first important explorations of the Mississippi Valley. Jean Nicolet, the French explorer, generally is credited with being the first Frenchman of New France to have picked up rumors of the Mississippi's existence. He heard such talk during an expedition to the Green Bay area. Some sources indicate that Pierre d'Espirit, Sieur des Raddison, and his brother-in-law, Médard Chouart, Sieur des Groseilliers (or so he called himself), the founders of the Hudson's Bay Company, discovered the river. They might have stepped across it near its source, not realizing it was any different from any other creek.

Despite all claims to the contrary, it would seem that the discoverers of the Mississippi were indeed Marquette and Joliet.

At that time, Louis XIV wanted a passage to Asia badly enough to pay a rich reward for it. Joliet (1645-1700) sought such an adventure, and Marquette saw in it an opportunity to win thousands of converts to Christianity. They elected to follow up those Indian rumors of a great river leading to the Vermillion Sea (the Pacific Ocean).

The twenty-seven-year-old Joliet met Marquette at St. Ignace (in what became Michigan) on December 8, 1672. They spent the rest of the winter there gathering whatever information the Indians could give them. On May 17, 1673, they and five French companions left in two light bark canoes. Traveling along the shore of Lake Michigan, they picked up two Miami guides and turned into Green Bay, following the Fox River through Lake Winnebago and on to the portage in central Wisconsin. There they carried their canoes to the Wisconsin River.

On June 17, 1673, they floated out onto the broad Mississippi, just downstream from present-day Prairie du Chien, Wisconsin. Marquette's journal contains abundant descriptions of the various phenomena of the river — Alton's Piasa bird, the confluence of the Missouri and the Mississippi, and the Chain of Rocks. Perhaps his most graphic description is of an area some miles below Ste. Genevieve:

> [We have reached] a place that is dreaded by the savages, because they believe that Manitou is there, that is to say, a demon, that devours travelers; and the savages, who wished to divert us from our undertaking, warned us against it. This is the demon: there is a small cove surrounded by rocks, 20 feet high, into which the whole current of the river rushes, and being pushed back against the waters following it, and checked by an island nearby, the current is compelled to pass through a narrow channel. This is not done without a violent struggle between these waters, which force one another back, or without a great din, which inspires terror in the savages, who fear everything.

Houck identifies this spot as Grand Tower, but more likely it is some long-vanished stretch of the Mississippi.

A short distance above the mouth of the Ohio River

they discovered an iron mine near some cliffs. "There are several veins of ore, and a bed a foot thick, and one sees large masses of it united with pebbles." This probably was the southeast corner of Perry County, just north of Apple Creek.

The explorers, apprehensive about the increased hostility of the Indians and running low on provisions, elected to return when they were near the mouth of the Arkansas River. By that time they had sound evidence that they were only a few days away from tidewater — not from the Vermillion Sea as they had hoped, but from the Gulf of Mexico.

They went back up the Illinois, and it was along this river that they found a village consisting of seventy-four cabins belonging to the Kaskaskia Indians of the Illinois confederation.

Marquette promised he would return and instruct them in Catholicism. On Holy Thursday 1675 he made his promise good, thus founding the famed mission of the Immaculate Conception — in what is now Starved Rock State Park in central Illinois.

His health broken, Marquette headed back to St. Ignace. Realizing he would never make it, he instructed his two Indian guides to pull into the mouth of a little river, now known as the Pere Marquette. There, at the age of thirty-eight, he died.

Joliet continued his explorations, but lost his journal of the Mississippi voyage in the Lachine rapids near Montreal. He became the official cartographer for New France.

While the goal of Marquette and Joliet was largely one of exploration, it fell to Robert Cavelier, Sieur de La Salle, to establish political claim to the vast Mississippi Valley for the House of Bourbon. Louis de

Buade, Comte de Frontenac, governor of New France, appointed La Salle to make the necessary voyage. With the approval of Louis XIV, La Salle assembled a party which included the daring one-armed Henri Tonti, the Franciscan Membre, and forty-four others, including women and children.

In December 1681 La Salle left Canada for the Gulf. He arrived at the Chicago River in January and moved down the Illinois to Starved Rock. There he found that the Kaskaskia village, which had contained 460 cabins in the fall of 1680, was all but deserted because of an attack by the Iroquois. He dragged his supplies across the ice of Lake Peoria and on February 6, 1682, he reached the Mississippi. Once there, he had to wait a week for the murderous ice floes to pass.

Continuing downstream the adventurer and his party reached the mouth of the Mississippi and tidewater on April 6, 1682, where he erected a cross on the site, thus officially claiming the valley, from the site of New Orleans to the site of Minneapolis-St. Paul, for his king.

La Salle had sent Louis Hennepin, a Franciscan, northward on the Mississippi in 1680, and it is believed the Hennepin company discovered the Falls of St. Anthony, at the site of the present-day Twin Cities.

La Salle found himself saddled with a change of superiors and fell into disfavor in Quebec. Taking matters into his own hands, he sailed for Versailles. Things were not going well for him in France either, until Hennepin's chronicles (full of wild exaggerations) appeared in print on the continent. With that, La Salle's fortunes rose, and he was given a fleet of four ships and some 280 persons so he could found a colony at the delta.

Back in New France Tonti heard of this good fortune and assembled a company to meet La Salle at the mouth of the Mississippi. La Salle never made it. He missed the delta by some 400 miles, due partly to the fact that the court had placed an unhappy captain in charge of the vessels. On December 19, 1658, the expedition sailed into Matagorda Bay, southwest of Galveston. The homesick captain took one of the two remaining ships and headed for Europe, leaving the angry La Salle to his own devices.

Still not knowing where he was, La Salle built another Fort St. Louis as the base for his colony and then set out on a series of expeditions to try to find the Mississippi. During one of them he lost his only remaining ship, the *La Belle.*

On January 12, 1687, La Salle left twenty persons at the fort and took the remaining twenty-eight with him on a final search for the river. On March 19, 1687, he was taunted into ambush and shot by two of his own men. The loyal remnants of the party eventually reached Quebec after La Salle's death had been avenged. (The colony was wiped out by Indians in 1689.)

It should be mentioned that La Salle deserved little blame for faulty navigation. The first practical chronometer was not to appear until 1735, and until that time an error of several thousand miles in cartography was not unheard of. Navigators of that day were adept at determining north-south positions. The angle between Polaris and the horizon corresponds (within about sixty miles) to the number of degrees of latitude north of the equator.

Longitude, however, was another matter. The contemporary celestial navigator can note the exact time of high noon with a chronometer which has been set at high noon at some known point. The difference in hours, minutes, and seconds can readily be translated into nautical miles. The early navigators needed chronometers which retained reasonable accuracy over many months.

Tonti waited patiently at the gulf for several months, then started his journey back to Quebec. He left a detachment to meet La Salle at the mouth of the Arkansas — that was the beginning of the old Arkansas Post.

Joutel, one of the survivors of the La Salle expedition, made note of both the Saline and of the high cliffs above Ste. Genevieve as he carried the news of the explorer's murder north.

> We held our way 'till the 25th [August 1687] when the indians showed us a spring of salt water within a musket-shot of us, and made us go ashore to view it. We observed the ground about it was much beaten by bullocks' feet, and it is likely that they love that salt water. . . .
>
> We proceeded on our journey the 28th and 29th, coasting along the foot of an upright rock about sixty or eighty feet high, around which the river glides. . . .
>
> The country was full of hillocks, covered with oak and walnut trees, abundance of plum trees, almost all the plums red and pretty good; besides, great stores of other sorts of fruits whose names we know not, and among them one shaped like middling pear, with stones in it as large as a bead. When ripe, it peels like a ripe peach, taste is of indifferent good, but rather of the sweetest.

La Salle, on his voyage back from the gulf in 1683,

paused long enough to establish Fort St. Louis along the Illinois River at Starved Rock. The scattered Kaskaskia Indians in the area reassembled nearby to form what became known as the Grand Village of the Kaskaskia. With other tribes La Salle and Tonti were able to entice into the area, the city enjoyed a population of more than 18,000.

Claude Allouez, S.J., inherited the Kaskaskia mission upon the death of Marquette, but was unable to erect a chapel during his ten years of service, largely because of La Salle's antagonism toward the Jesuits.

The site was abandoned about 1691 because the dense population had denuded the surrounding area of trees and game. The next spring the community was reestablished at the lower end of Lake Peoria, where the second Fort St. Louis was constructed. Soon there were three chapels serving the Indian city.

Because of internal dissensions, the Kaskaskia elected to part from the Peoria Indians. With the Jesuit Jacques Gravier scouting ahead, they moved down the Illinois. Gabriel Marest, another Jesuit, brought them by way of Cahokia to the mouth of *La Riviere Des Peres,* the southern boundary of present-day St. Louis, where they remained from 1700 to 1703. While there they were joined by most of the Tamaroa Indians and a few Frenchmen from Cahokia.

Prior to that time the Tamaroa and Cahokia Indians had established neighboring villages at Cahokia, across the Mississippi from St. Louis. Here three priests from the seminary at Quebec established their mission to the Tamaroa in 1699. They were Jean François Buisson de St. Cosme, François Joliet de Montigny, and Antoine Davion — known to history as the Gentlemen of the Seminary.

In 1700 the Kaskaskia and a third of the Tamaroa moved to River Des Peres and the mission became known as the Cahokias. In the spring of 1703 the settlement moved down the Mississippi River to the Kaskaskia River, pulled upstream a few miles, and on the southwest side of the river they founded Kaskaskia, with the noted Marest as their missionary.

Kaskaskia rapidly became a center of trade for the area. Built around a large square, the narrow streets divided the land into blocks of four lots each. Wheat was introduced by the Jesuits. Oats, hemp, corn, garden vegetables, hops, and tobacco also were grown. The Indians pursued their old ways alongside the whites until 1719, when most of them were relocated four or five miles up the Kaskaskia River.

Back in Cahokia, the Gentlemen of the Seminary were in the rather awkward position of being missionaries without having anyone to preach to. They struck out downstream, going as far as Tonti's Arkansas Post, then returned to established villages where they were wanted and needed. St. Cosme, the most literate of the three, left this account of the Grand Tower, a startling landmark some forty miles downstream from Ste. Geneviève:

> There is a rock on the right which advances into the river and forms an island, or rather a rock 200 feet high, which, making the river turn back very rapidly and entering the channel, forms a kind of whirlpool there, where it is said a canoe was engulfed at the high waters. Fourteen Miamis were once lost there, which has rendered the spot fearful among the Indians, so that they are accustomed to make some sacrifices to this rock when they pass. You ascend this island and rock by a hill with considerable difficulty. On it we

planted a beautiful cross, singing the "Vexilla Regis," and our people fired three volleys of musketry.

The ensuing years saw more and more Frenchmen come into the Middle Valley. With such colonization came a need for local civil and military rule, to protect both the interests and the lives of the settlers.

It was late in 1718 when Pierre Duque de Boisbriant, newly appointed commandant of the Illinois country, arrived at Kaskaskia with orders to erect a military post. He selected a site on the east bank some eighteen miles to the north and built a strong wood stockade, which was reinforced with the earth removed when a moat was dug. That was the first Fort de Chartres, which was completed in 1720.

The fort was built too near the river and the reinforcing soon ended up at New Orleans. Rebuilt in 1727, it was in such disrepair only five years later that the commandant ordered another new fort built some distance from the flood waters. This structure, which now has been restored, was begun in 1753 and completed three years later. It was supposed to have been the best-built fort in North America and was to be the last French fortification on the continent to lower the lilies of France.

In 1712 Antoine Crozat, one of the wealthiest merchants in France, was granted a charter which allowed him to open the commerce of Louisiana. With Antoine de la Mothe Cadillac in charge, the expedition aborted early. The Spaniards had no intention of cooperating with the venture.

Their charter was surrendered in 1717 to the "Company of the West," which soon was united with the Company of the Indies to become the Royal Company of the Indies. None of these achieved any real success.

There is little documentation to support this, but it appears as if Mine La Motte, located near County Road 00 about sixteen miles southeast of Farmington, was opened by Cadillac and was the result of a very bad practical joke. Joseph Schlarman reports in *From Quebec to New Orleans* that in 1714 a man named Du Tisné brought to Governor Cadillac two samples of ore which he stated came from an area near Kaskaskia. A quiet assay proved an unusually high silver content, so Cadillac left for the Illinois Country to investigate. The Cadillac party left Kaskaskia and journeyed several miles up the Saline, then over to Big River, a tributary of the Meramec. Cadillac opened a pit about four feet deep, down to rock. Finding northing to excite them but lead ore, they packed up their tools and went home to Mobile in October 1715. There is reason to believe this was the beginning of the celebrated Mine la Motte. Cadillac learned later that the ore samples had been given to Du Tisne by a visitor from Mexico.

CHAPTER IV.

The Founding of Ste. Genevieve

Many of the earliest American towns were founded because of the strategic advantages of the terrain — strategic as a military defense or as a protected port. Until the publication of Carl G. Ekberg's *Colonial Ste. Genevieve* (1985, Patrice Press) it had been believed that Ste. Genevieve is where it is because the terrain delivers easy access to the Mississippi River. It was the closest point to the mines some miles inland — not the deposits of precious metals sought with such determination by the conquistadors, but veins of lead of incredible richness. So extensive are the deposits that the area still is being worked and still is producing in substantial quantities.

Philip François Renault, a wealthy Paris banker, was appointed director-general of the mining operations of the Royal Company of the Indies. Henry Rowe Schoolcraft, writing in 1819, dates the Renault appointment exactly one century earlier, in 1719. He states that Renault left France that year with 200 miners and laborers and all the needed provisions and picked up some 500 Guinea blacks from Santo

Domingo during the voyage to Kaskaskia. He added that Renault arrived there in 1720. Much of that information, along with the reason for founding Ste. Genevieve, has been proved untrue. Renault had twenty-two black slaves. There were thirteen whites, including him.

Schoolcraft was a reporter writing partially from observation and partially from hearsay, and he neglected to mention which was which. Houck, the noted Missouri historian, wrote in 1908 that Renault arrived in Kaskaskia in 1723, a date which also has considerable backing from other historians. This position is supported by the late Francis J. Yealy, S.J., one of the early historians of Ste. Genevieve.

Houck stated that Renault even brought the bricks for his furnaces from France, each identified with his name. This may have been true — a surveyor named Cozzens is reported to have uncovered such a brick around 1900 while working near *Fourche à Renault* in Washington County, where one of Renault's furnaces was constructed. On the other hand, brick kilns are not that difficult to construct, and it is possible that the bricks were formed and fired in the area.

It had been thought that Ste. Genevieve could have been founded within months after the arrival of Renault, and not in 1735.

Renault temporarily established his company in the old settlement of St. Ann, near Fort de Chartres. This served until he could get a new stone house erected just outside the walls. He named his concession town St. Philippe. (St. Ann later was washed away by the Mississippi.)

Renault reopened Mine La Motte and is believed to have developed the lead mines of Washington County.

He housed his specialists in a long-disappeared settlement known as *Cabanage à Renaudière.* By 1725 he was producing 1,500 pounds of lead per day.

The mining techniques were primitive, but the ore was so rich that the profits were substantial. Pickaxes, shovels, drills, rammers, and priming rods for blasting were the tools of the trade. The men would measure off an eight-foot square, digging down to ten, twelve, or even fifteen feet — as far as a good man could throw the dirt and ore. Then they would go deeper, rigging a windlass to haul the ore to the surface.

The spar was cleaned with a pointed pick, then broken into fist-size hunks weighing about fifteen pounds. A 5,000-pound charge of ore would be placed in a U-shaped brick furnace lined on the inside and front with logs. The ore was heated slowly for twelve hours to rid it of sulphur, then brought to smelting temperatures for another twelve hours. Three-man crews would cart the wood day and night. The yield was about fifty percent pure lead.

Ida M. Schaaf, writing in the *Missouri Historical Review* in 1933, tried to establish the founding of Ste. Genevieve a good many years prior to the traditionally accepted date of 1735. She felt that the lead would have been brought to the river over *le grand champ,* just below present-day Ste. Genevieve. It might have been brought as far north as a mile or two above town, but upstream from there are cliffs of such formidability that it is improbable that a landing could have been made in that vicinity. It was said that the lead, molded in the shape of a thin horsecollar, was transported to the river around the necks and backs of horses. From Ste. Genevieve the mineral supposedly was placed on keelboats and shipped north to Fort de Chartres. There it was weighted and placed back on the boats for the port settlement of New Orleans, which in 1723 had been in existence only five years. The logic is incredible.

Schaaf admits the improbability of all this. There seems to be no logical reason for fighting the Mississippi current some twelve miles with a heavy load, only to retrace immediately the route on the way to the gulf.

Nothing could have been done in Fort de Chartres that couldn't have been done more efficiently on the west bank, and Schaaf felt that Renault, being a businessman, must have known this. She found it illogical that the dispatchers and weighers would have returned to Fort de Chartres each night, and it is also improbable that they lived on the keelboats until they received their full loads, when dry land was only a few feet away. Therefore, she felt that they must have erected some small cabins, and if they did, that was the start of Ste. Genevieve. Any records that might have been kept have yet to be discovered. But the assumption was made that Ste. Genevieve was founded about 1723, not in 1735.

Father Yealy cited a number of dates, each having some documentation. He wrote of two old maps dated 1755, bearing the legend, "French Village founded 3. years ago." This would establish the founding in 1752, provided the period didn't indicate decades, or thirty years. In that case it would be 1722.

Philibert F. Watrin, S.J., one of the priests banished during the Jesuit expulsion in 1763 and 1764, served Ste. Genevieve from Kaskaskia. During his exile in France the Blackrobe wrote: "Fifteen years ago, at a ·league from the old village, on the other bank of the Mississippi, there was established a new village under

the name of Sainte Genevieve.'' That would set the
date in the late 1740s. This dating happens to be ex-
traordinarily accurate. Capt. Philip Pittman in 1767
wrote: ''The first settlers of this village removed from
Cascassquias about 28 years ago,'' or in 1739.
Wrong.

In 1881 the crumbling bank of the Mississippi at *le
grand champ* exposed the ruins of an old well. One of the
stones bore the date 1732.

One of Father Yealy's most significant finds was a
document dated May 25, 1732, in which Father
Mercier, head of the Cahokia mission, addressed to the
seminary at Quebec: ''Scarcely a month ago I had the
honor to send you with a certain Louis Poulin from the
parish of Saint Joachim, all the papers and documents
that will help you, etc.'' Yealy felt that, since St.
Joachim was the early name of the Ste. Genevieve
parish, it would appear that by the date there was more
there than a cabin or two. He reasoned that, while it
definitely wasn't a parish by canon law at that time, it
was an actual settlement large enough to be assigned a
patron.

Charles E. Peterson, the noted architectural
historian, states that the village was among the first in
Missouri, after the old River des Peres (1700), and
along with Cabanage à Renaudière (1720), Mine La
Motte, Mines of the Meramec, and Fort d'Orleans, all
1723; Mine à Renault, 1724-25; and Vielles (Old)
Mines, 1726.

One of the most valued documents in the archives of
the Missouri Historical Society is a certified copy of
Hunt's ''Minutes.'' Theodore Hunt was a recorder of
land titles, commissioned by the American govern-

ment to travel the villages around St. Louis, obtaining depositions to be used as confirmation of Spanish land grants. Hunt often added to his minutes information which he thought was important and yet had nothing to do with the job at hand.

In Book II, page 206, appears the following notation:

Julien Labriere being duly sworn, says He is fifty Six years of age, and that he was born in the old village of S'Genevieve, which place was built about where the lower ferry is at present, that when He first had any recollection, He remembers seeing A man then very old named Baptiste LaRose, who was the first settler in the Old Village (this man died when he was One hundred & three years old) about fifty years ago there was fifty or Sixty Cabens in the old village — about forty one years ago, the Bank having caved in very much, compelled the Inhabitants to think of removing from the Old Village, and A D One thousand seven hundred and Eighty four three men named Loisel, Maurice Chatillon and Jacque Boyer removed from the old village and established the present village of S'Genevieve and they built houses on the lots at present occupied by Grifford, Daget and Veuve Leclere, Oro was the then Commandant — the following the year after the commencement of the settlement of the new village was l'anee Des Grande Eaus, the old village was overflowed, so as to be on the top of the houses — A boat of Mr Chouteaus arrived at this time and they made the Boat fast to the Top of one of the Chimneys, and dived on the roof of the house — in the Big field the water in many places was twelve or fifteen feet deep —

his

Julien   **X**   Labriere

mark

Sworn to before me October 22d 1825—
Theodore Hunt Recorder LT.''

There could be some truth in the statement that La
Rose was the first settler in the town. "Very old"
could have been eighty, and "first . . . recollection"
could have been at age ten, which would have put La
Rose's birth date about 1699. Thus, he could have
been about twenty-four in 1723, when Renault was in
the area. Could La Rose have been one of the dispatchers who loaded the lead on Renault's keelboats?
Could he have been the builder of a cabin on the bank,
to provide shelter on dry land and serve as some sort of
office? The answers to all those questions are now
known, and they are all the same — no. Carl Ekberg,
after years of intense research, was unwilling to accept
all the old wives' tales. One by one, he proved them
untrue or ridiculously illogical. For instance, Renault
was close to a number of rivers flowing into the
Mississippi. It makes no sense at all to presume that he
would transport the heavy ore overland for dozens of
miles when it could be placed upon small boats and
floated downstream to the Mississippi.

Then Ekberg set about proving that Ste. Genevieve
was founded by Kaskaskia farmers, seeking rich lands
to replace their worn-out fields on the east bank. The
French were good record keepers — nothing appears

on the land records until 1749. From then on the records appear with growing regularity. Ste. Genevieve was founded in the late 1740s. There can no longer be any question about it.

CHAPTER V.

Silver Spoons on the Frontier

The village of Ste. Genevieve probably began with merely a cabin or two, but few could survive alone in the hostile wilderness. Banding together for the common defense became necessary. The Osage Indians would think nothing of a 100-mile trek if the reward involved a fine horse, beef, cattle, or sheep. They weren't killers, but they were among the world's most brazen thieves.

The settlers built their homes with this in mind. Individual properties were laid out in squares about the size of a small city block. Enclosing the square was a stockade fence of vertically-placed pointed logs, usually cedar or oak, about seven feet high. About three feet of the log was buried in the ground. The houses usually faced the river and were situated very close to the fence. In back of the house were three or four structures — a kitchen and bake house, a smokehouse, an outhouse, and a well. The well often was made of stone, with a small wood truss overhead which, like the house, was covered with thatch. The bucket was lowered from a small windlass.

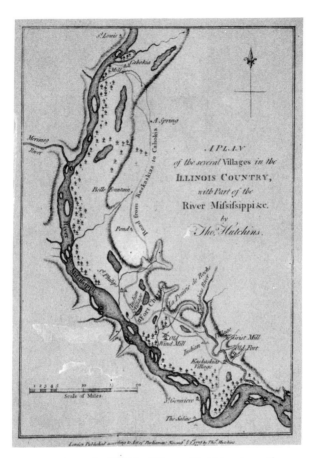

A map drawn in 1771 by Thomas Hutchins shows the area later known as the American Bottom. Hutchins said that the communities there had populations of "1273 sencible men." He counted 208 French and 80 Negroes in Ste. Genevieve then.

Thatched roofs were common in Ste. Genevieve until about 1800, when they gave way to hand-split shingles, which afforded greater resistance to fire.

The balance of the building lot was usually used for growing the vegetables needed to sustain the family for a year. Herb gardens were commonplace. Their yield was used as medicine and as spices. Grapevines were the source of good wines, so satisfying to the French palate. Fruit trees often were planted. Some of the town lots had areas where livestock could be tethered — even barns — in the event of warnings of Indian attacks.

The map drawn in 1771 by Thomas Hutchins shows the area later known as the American Bottom. Hutchins said that communities there had a population of "1273 sencible men." He counted 208 French and eighty blacks in Ste. Genevieve then.

The houses themselves often were one-room units, sometimes two, but seldom more. Typical exterior dimensions were 12' × 13', 15' square, and 18' × 19'. They usually were made of logs placed vertically into the ground, five or six inches apart. Such construction was called *poteaux en terre* — posts in the ground. A few houses had rubble stone foundations on which the ends of the logs rested — *poteaux sur solle* — posts on a sill. The walls were tilted inward a few degrees, for stability. The interstices were filled with *bouzillage* — a mixture which incorporated clay or mud, plus a binder of twigs, animal hair, straw, or limestone gravel.

The ceilings of the houses sometimes were planked, but never plastered. Ceiling beams usually were exposed. The overhead sometimes served as sleeping quarters for the children of large families. Often the roof was raised to provide a crawl space between the top of the wall and the underside of the roof. This proved an ideal vantage point for defense against livestock raids by the Indians, giving the occupants an opportunity to fire over the stockade and providing a sort of linear loophole for protection against returned fire.

The walls of the house usually were plastered, and there was a limestone fireplace in every room. Iron and glass were rarities and had to be imported from France. Solid shutters and gates swung on hook-and-eye hinges. There probably was no glass in Ste. Genevieve windows in its first years.

Frequently the earth beneath the center of a house was removed to form a cellar for the storage of fruit and vegetables grown in the garden.

The center area of the larger houses served as a large entrance hall. A room on one side was a combination living and dining room, and sleeping quarters were on the other side. The exterior walls always were whitewashed, partly to protect the *bouzillage* and partly to reflect the heat. (Whitewash was produced by burning limestone.)

In the early years the houses were patterned after those in Quebec and Normandy. But Ste. Genevieve is some 600 miles farther south than either area, and settlers found the heat in the Middle Valley oppressive. The French planters who settled the area brought with them the idea of the *galerie* — a wide porch which was added to all four sides of a house.

Many architectural authorities credit the *galerie* to the pioneer French of Santo Domingo. Ernest Allen Connally, chief of the Office of Archaeology and Historic Preservation of the National Park Service, states that the *galerie* actually originated in sixteenth century France. Since the rooms usually were arranged *en suite* in Normandy, the *galerie* was used as a corridor. The New World development seems to have been the enlargement of the European *galerie,* which extended completely around the house. One of its main functions was to keep the sun and the rain off the whitewashed walls.

As thatch was displaced by more fire-resistant materials, the kitchens were moved up under the *galeries* and the cooking was done in the house proper, without excessive danger of fire.

The houses and lots of old Ste. Genevieve were strung out along the riverbank for more than a mile. There was no evidence of a common stockade wall — evidently each owner left a lane on all sides of his property. There was little land planning; the houses were strung out helter-skelter rather than in an orderly grid. Some houses were located two or three ''blocks'' from the river.

Behind the cluster of stockades stood *le grand champ* — 3,000 acres of alluvium. There was no common ownership in Ste. Genevieve. Each family had its own piece of ground. This is unlike many other frontier settlements, where agricultural production was divided among the families in accordance with their need. The land was divided into arpents — a measure of both area and linearity. An arpent, or ''arp,'' measured about 192′6″. Most of the lots in the field were one arp wide and stretched back almost a mile to the little road at the foot of the limestone bluff, now known as the St. Marys road. There was another road bisecting the field, from the bluff to the river.

Records of the elaborate fence regulations are abundant in the archives of the Missouri Historical Society. A common fence paralleled the river, another the St. Marys road. Individual fences separated one tract from another and were designed more to identify boundaries than to secure the crops against the wild and domestic animals that roamed the woods in *le domaine du roy* — the surrounding property held in the name of the king — from which additional land grants were made. Pecan trees were planted on *le grand champ* to mark the lot lines, and a few are still alive today.

It was the job of the civil commandant to enforce the fence regulations, infractions of which were punishable by stiff fines and jail sentences.

Cattle, sheep, and horses all were branded and roamed the king's land freely, often wandering into town, up and down the twisted little lanes. They frequently were wintered on the little river islands to keep them from moving off into the wilderness.

Corn, pumpkins, wheat, oats, barley, flax, cotton, and tobacco were products of the big field. The settlers, hampered by the lack of steel implements, usually planted the fields and left them alone until harvest time.

There were one or two wood harrows, the property of the village. Although records of early years are scarce, the wheat crop in one year was not enough to supply the colony and added supplies had to be imported. The yield may have been terrible, but they had a ball all summer long.

There was game for the shooting: wild turkeys, geese, ducks, swans, pelicans, quail, pigeons, eagles, and turkey buzzards — by the thousands. If the Mississippi didn't cooperate with fish, there was always meat.

The pioneers used horses, oxen, and boats for transportation. The heavy loads were carried in four-wheeled wagons; two-wheeled carts (charettes) were for human transport only. Oxen, yoked at the horns, provided power for the heaviest loads and were directed by whips instead of reins. Tough little ponies pulled the charettes. There was no steel or iron in Ste. Genevive in its first years. It wasn't until the late 1800s that wood wheels were fitted with iron tires. Many of the vehicles had chairs strapped to their sides for the comfort of women and children.

The people of Ste. Genevieve were different from the colonizers of the Eastern seaboard. Capt. Amos Stoddard, who claimed Upper Louisiana for the United States after the Louisiana Purchase, stated that in no other country was aggravated crime more rare than in Louisiana. "The art of deception, when calculated to work injury, is scarcely known among them . . . they are never so unhappy as when in debt, and never more happy then released from apprehension of a legal process."

Ward A. Dorrance had an opportuntiy to spend a summer in the early 1930s in the town of Old Mines, the site of Mine Renault and Mine à Breton. Of the 600 families in the Catholic parish at that time, ninety percent still used French as the domestic tongue. In the village, about forty miles west of Ste. Genevieve, it was at that late date possible to gain a glimpse of life as it must have existed 200 years earlier in Ste. Genevieve.

The men worked in the mines and fields Mondays and Tuesdays from dawn until dark, in hopes of getting enough work done by noon Wednesday so they could take the next four days off. If so, they would play cards, dance, sing, or gather together to see who could spin the tallest tales.

Their lightheartedness was reflected in the nicknames they gave each other and for other towns, many of them unprintable. Ste. Genevieve, as has been said, was nicknamed *Misére* — miserable. Kaskaskia was *Pouilleux* — lousy. Cape Girardeau was *L'anse à la Graisse* — greasy cove. Cardondelet, where one of the attractions was a race track, was *Vide-Poche* — empty pocket. St Louis was *Paincourt* — short of bread.

Nicknames were especially popular with the settlers. One of the aged Old Mines storytellers was nicknamed *Gros Vaisse,* and the reader may look that up, since this is intended to be a family book. These names were not used behind a person's back — they were used openly and still are. Those who bear them would think something was wrong if they were called by their legal name.

The custom persists in Ste. Genevieve today. There is Punkin' Basler, Fuclos La Rose, Horse Maurice, Flakes Bahr, Toothpick Bollinger, Possum Grass, Beck Basler, Bigfoot Basler (and his son Young Bigfoot Basler), and an entire family bearing the names of Izzy, Dizzy, Nuts, Boats, and Nooney. The prominent Sexauer family includs men nicknamed Guinea, Sleepy, Funny, and Grandpa. One man has his nickname, "Boob," painted on his mailbox and listed in the Ste. Genevieve telephone directory. Some of those names are attached to the town's leading citizens.

The national insults were plentiful, particularly after the French population was augmented by those from other national orgins. There was the Blue Bellied Yankee — with "land so poor his belly turned blue." And the pawpaw Frenchmen, who had to "live off

pawpaws in the summer and 'possums in the winter.''
A man's wife was the ''old lady,'' a term accepted by
both sexes. After the arrival of the Germans, a fight
could be precipitated simply by shouting, ''Damn the
Deutch!''

People found their way around not by following
marked highways, but by knowing the hollows. Each
one had its name. They still do, and any good Ste.
Genevieve County farmer can rattle them off one by
one — Blue Jug Hollow, Snell Hollow, Red Barn
Hollow, Bowes Hollow, and others.

The pronunciation of the ''Missouri French'' was
rugged at best. When Americans and Germans applied
their influence it was all but unintelligible. *Fourche Du
Clos* (Bloomsdale) became Fusch Da Clew. *Bois Brule*
Bottom became Bob Rudy Bottom. *Isle Du Bois*
became, of all things, Zillaboy. *Aux Arcs* became
Ozarks.

While some early observers spoke of Ste. Genevieve
in charitable terms, this wasn't always the case. Don
Pedro Piernas, military commandant in the early days
of St. Louis, reported that the people of Ste. Genevieve
were characterized by a ''looseness of conduct, the
abandonment of life . . . dissoluteness and license.''

Perrin du Lac, writing in the 1790s, said that the
children were ''without learning or desire of learning.
The youth spend their time riding, hunting, dancing.
The children have contracted the manners and
insolence of the natives.''

Despite the allegations of the bluenosed, the people
of Ste. Genevieve were kind, gentle, and highly
cultured. They were honest and scrupulous. There
were laws, but few of them were written down. The
epitome of disgrace was legal punishment of any kind.

The manners of the townspeople were elegant. Wives were the full partners of their husbands. Slaves usually were treated, to some extent, as members of the family. Balls sometimes lasted continuously for two or three days. Slaves and Indians were invited to attend, and they came. So did the children, from toddlers on up.

While even the lowliest Americans were filled with prejudices — against Indians, blacks, and other nationalities — the French hardly knew the meaning of the word.

Their food was sophisticated, too, as much so as the frontier would allow. Elaborate soups were prepared, and fricassees, salads, chicken, and wild game. The French palate would tolerate none of the crude corn-pone and fat hog meat of the American.

One of the most colorful customs in North America — *La Guisgnolée* — was brought to the Middle Valley and Ste. Genevieve by the French. It survives today only in isolated sections of rural France and Canada and in Ste. Genevieve. It was revived in the 1970s in old Cahokia.

In the old days, the young men of the village went from house to house on New Year's Eve dressed in outlandish costumes, dancing a shuffling little step and singing a song to the accompaniment of two or three fiddles. The music, due to erratic tempo variations and a lack of voicing, would be all but impossible to set on paper. It has strong Gregorian overtones, and probably has come down from the middle ages almost intact.

During *La Guignolée*, the performers, blacked as Negroes or browned as Indians, would go from house to house begging food, which they would store for a banquet on Twelfth Night. At the banquet the young men took slices of a cake into which one bean had been baked. The man who got the bean was entitled to take a girl of his choice to the ball which followed.

The custom continues today in Ste. Genevieve. The singers are content to be invited into the various homes on their itinerary for a drink. Native Frenchmen have heard recordings of the Ste. Genevieve *La Guignolée* singers and have been unable to understand a single word. This probably is because the lustiest of the performers today are German and can't comprehend a word of French themselves. But they sing *La Guignolée* anyway. Tradition is tradition in Ste. Genevieve.

The lyric is as follows:

La Guignolée

Bonsoir le maître et la maîtresse
　　Et tout le monde du logis!
Pour le premier jour de l'année
La Guignolée nous vous devez.
　　Si vous n'avez rien à nous donner
Dites-nous le!
　　Nous vous, demandons pas grand 'chose
Une échinée
　　Une échinée n'est pas grand 'chose
De quatre-vingt dix pieds le long;
　　Encore nous demandons pas grand 'chose,
La fille ainée de la maison
　　Nous lui ferons faire bonne chère
　　Nous lui ferons chauffer les pieds
Nous salvons la compagnie
　　Et la prions nous excuser.
Si l'on à fait quelque folie
　　C'étoit pour nous des ennuyer

Une autre fois nous prendons garde
    Quand sera temps d'y revenir
Dansons la Guenille, dansons la Guenille, dansons
    la Guenille!

    Chorus

Bonsoir le maître et la maîtresse
    Et tout le monde du logis!

Ensemble:

Good evening master and mistress,
    and to everyone else who lives with you.
For the first day of the year,
    You owe us *La Guignolée*
If you have nothing at all to give,
    Tell us of it right away.
We're not asking for very much,
    A chine of meat or so will do.
A chine of meat is not a big thing,
    only ninety feet long.
Again, we're not asking for very much,
    only the oldest daughter of the house.
We will give her lots of good cheer,
    and we will surely warm her feet.
Now, we greet your company,
    and beg you to forgive us please.
If we have acted a little crazy,
    we only meant it in good fun.

Another time we'll surely be careful
    to know when we must come back here again.
Let us dance la Guenille, la Guenille, la Guenille!

Chorus

Good evening master and mistress
    and to everyone else who lives with you!

In the earliest days, the people of the little village
lived like the Indians. They sent their furs and other
goods downstream to a factor, who traded them for
whatever was needed or possible to get from the French
export trade. With the burgeoning growth of New
Orleans, trading became easier and the villagers began
acquiring some of the trappings that they had known in
the old country.

Gradually they developed currency — "carrots" of
tobacco, furs, and finally Mexican coins. (The
"carrot" was a roll of tobacco which had been ham-
mered into a half-inch hole in a log. The log then was
split and the hard "carrot" extracted.)

Some of the citizens of Ste. Genevieve prospered
and enjoyed their incomes enormously. One example
of the extent of an individual's personal possessions is
found in the will of Jacques Louis Lambert *dit* (known
as) Lafleur, a merchant and militia officer who died the
day after Christmas 1771. He left a regimental coat
and vest, sword and belt, gun and powerhorn, gold
watch worth 200 livres (about $25), gold button, silver
snuffbox, three pairs of silver buckles, a silver cross,

silver spoon, silver fork, two silver rings, a hunting knife, two purses, two looking glasses, a hat, an Indian pipe, twenty-two shirts, twelve night caps, thirty handkerchiefs, six drawers, two umbrellas, two mattresses, a featherbed, a blanket, a bed curtain, a pillowcase, three cravats, three tablecloths, eight pairs of breeches, a candlestick, a yardstick, a brush, a powder bag, a clock, a muff, a capot, a curling iron, plates, a tureen, several bottles, a basket, a bowl, pots, a copper kettle, a barrel, a birdcage, deerskins, and "other property."

The great expansion of trade which made such personal property possible also provided a voluminous source of daydreams for the youngsters in Ste. Genevieve. If they tired of dreaming of guiding expeditions to the West, they could always dream of the life of a river boatman.

It may have been glamorous to the young boys, but such a livelihood was quite another matter to the men who had to do the work. Canoes, pirogues, and flat boats were used in the New Orleans trade. The flat boats weighed twenty to thirty tons and generally were scrapped in New Orleans, with the complement of ten men and their patron making their way back afoot.

The keelboats, weighing fifty to sixty tons, were too expensive to break down at the delta. They were equipped with masts and sails, and had tolerable living accommodations aboard for the patron and his crew of forty to fifty men. Generally boats were equipped with a rudder. They moved about a mile an hour against the current. When stuck on a bar, the deckhands would move in circles around the deck, straining against their long poles. The trip back from New Orleans often took two months.

While truly magnificent imports from Europe were available to those in the Middle Valley who were willing to wait for them, not many could afford the cost. There were more poor people than rich people in Ste. Genevieve as everywhere else. Deman Detailly, an Indian interpreter who married a squaw, left in his will a featherbed covered with skins, another with ticking, four delft plates, a tin pan, a shovel, seven pewter spoons, four iron forks, an adz, saw, oven, table, four chairs, two sheets, two pairs of cotton breeches, one shirt, a blanket, a straw hat, and a pair of mittens.

The men of early Ste. Genevieve, almost without exception, wore their hair in long queues. It was held by an eelskin — a band used both to keep the hair off the back of the neck and to keep perspiration from dripping into their eyes. They wore coarse linen pantaloons, moccasins, and a blanket coat with cape, which fitted over the head. Men and women alike wore blue bandannas over their heads. Men of peasant lineage, who could not afford articles of cloth, often dressed completely in buckskins which they made themselves. The coats of men of substance were often made in Paris and were adorned with intricate designs of gold and silver braid and ornamented with solid silver buttons.

The peasant women, like the men, wore moccasins. They generally dressed in voluminous skirts of bold-patterned materials. Frequently their aprons were made of plain deerskin.

Women of wealth often had several corsets from France, silk scarves, combs of horn and ivory, and silk stockings. As soon as the New Orleans importers started operating in full swing, these ladies were able to procure plenty of serge, linen, silk, taffeta, satin, and velvet.

Travelers in the mid-continent, used to the roughness found east of the Mississippi, often were startled to find a compact, genteel civilization in the wilderness of the Middle Valley. They still are.

CHAPTER VI.

God and the Rolling Bones

The Mission of the Immaculate Conception in Kaskaskia was instrumental in the development of Ste. Genevieve from the beginning. It is believed that a church was erected on *le grand champ* about 1752. In that year, a François Rivard petitioned for land in *le grand champ* and promised to donate some of it for a church.

Certainly in the beginning the religious needs of the community had to be administered by priests from Kaskaskia, which necessitated an upstream pull of three or four miles. It may be presumed that the village received priestly visitations several times a year, and it also may be presumed that whoever did the rowing must have wanted a church there badly.

The first regular pastor was a Jesuit named Jean Baptiste de la Morinie, and it is his name that appears on all the records from November 10, 1761, to October 15, 1763, the year of the infamous Jesuit expulsion from French America. The earliest record is February 26, 1759, noting the marriage of Andre de Guire, *dit* La Rose, and Marie La Boissiere, the widow of Joseph Baron.

Missionary priests who, being quartered in Kaskaskia, might have visited the settlement, include François Louis Vivier, 1714-1756; François J. B. Aubert, 1722-1785(?); Philibert Watrin, 1697-1765(?); and Alexis F. X. DeGuyenne, 1696-1762. The Jesuit Joseph Gagnon and a Franciscan, Luc Collet, also could have ministered to Ste. Genevieve. The records indicate that another early pastor was J. B. F. Salveneuve, 1708-1764.

In light of the recreative activities of the early days, some might find it difficult to believe there was any religious influence in the community at all. Christian Schultz, writing early in the nineteenth century, had this to say about the situation:

> Whenever there is a ball given even by the most rigid of these Catholics, there is always one room set apart for gambling. And never did I see people embark with so much spirit and perseverance to win each other's money as in this little village. They spend 30 hours at the same table with only claret and coffee, and exclusive of these frequent opportunities . . . they have meetings thrice a week for no other purpose than to play their favorite game . . . Should the billiard rooms, of which there are three, be closed the whole week, you will always see them open and crowded on Sunday.

Where was the Church during all this so-called debauchery? Right in the middle of it, still playing a constructive role. The rugged, kindly priests had taught their lessons well. The pioneer French were gamblers, but there is nothing in the records to show that there was widespread gambling to excess. They saw nothing immoral in dancing on Sunday. The priests went along with this because there was no reason not to. While Don Pedro Piernas (lieutenant governor of Upper Louisiana), declared that the people of Ste. Genevieve were characterized by "license, laxity of conduct and vice," it should be noted that Piernas and his company were from a land where instances of rank bigotry, lawsuits, and capital crimes were matters of course. The people of Ste. Genevieve were listening to a different drummer — and a better one.

Almost all the credit for the sophistication of the citizens of early Ste. Genevieve is attributable to the influence of the Roman Catholic Church. The frontier priests and missionaries were strict enough to command and receive general adherence to the basic laws of the outdated customs of Europe which often made little sense in the New World. Each man and woman was a full-fledged citizen of the community, receiving all rights and accepting all responsibilities. Why was gambling allowed? Because citizens usually feared the social disgrace of pauperism more than they coveted the winnings of the gaming table. Long before the losses could approach a critical amount, an unlucky gambler left the games for home and hearth.

The Church did not require sacrifice from the devout frontiersman. Social pressures demanded that each family give as much as it could afford to give and no more. This usually was enough to sustain the priests and missionaries. Under Spanish rule the crown paid the clergy in large measure. Only once in the early years did a priest (François Hilaire) try to extract the full ten percent tithe, and he was nearly run out of town. Carl J. Ekberg has a passage in his *Colonial Ste. Genevieve* which reveals that all was not always sweetness and light between priests and parishioners:

> Troubles between [Father] Hilaire [de Geneveaux] and his parishioners began almost immediately. In the

summer of 1774 the townspeople of Ste. Genevieve began to complain about their new pastor to Lieutenant Governor Piernas in St. Louis: Hilaire was demanding a literal tithe of one-tenth of his parishioners' incomes instead of the one-twenty-sixth that had been customary in all French colonies in North America. Hilaire was not instructing the youth in the faith and delivering sermons. Hilaire had forbidden his flock to see the priest from across the Mississippi (i.e., the popular Gibault). In June 1774 more than thirty citizens of Ste. Genevieve petitioned Piernas to straighten Hilaire out. The petitioners even suggested that the priest might wish to leave the parish; and, two months later, fifteen of the bolder citizens demanded outright that Hilaire be removed from Ste. Genevieve because he was an incorrigible troublemaker . . . Hilaire's peculiar personality blossomed out bizarrely in the affair of the missing church pew.

Both Louis Villars, town commandant, and François Vallé I, civil judge and commander of the local militia, had special pews installed at the front of the parish church in Ste. Genevieve. In June 1775 Vallé's pew came up missing. Villars, Vallé's son-in-law, reported to the new lieutenant governor in St. Louis, [Francisco] Cruzat, that Father Hilaire had spirited it away while Vallé was ill and indisposed. Cruzat must have wondered what on earth was going on down in Ste. Genevieve, but on July 3, 1775, he sent orders to both Villars and Hilaire that Vallé's pew would forthwith be returned to its customary place in the church. Cruzat already sensed that in the person of Father Hilaire he had a strange case on his hands and he begged the priest to "restrain yourself to avoid such scandals." Hilaire turned a deaf ear to Cruzat's plea however. Commandant Villars had soldiers from the Spanish garrison in Ste. Genevieve conduct a house to house (including the rectory) search for Vallé's pew, and the pew was found behind the rectory smashed to bits. Everyone knew that Hilaire was responsible for this outrage, but because there was no proof the cost of building Vallé a new pew was borne by general parish funds. Indeed, it is conceivable that disgruntled parishioners framed Hilaire in this case, although his future conduct would suggest that he was the guilty party. While Vallé's new pew was being built, Villars magnanimously turned his personal pew over to his aging father-in-law.

Hilaire eventually carried his dementia to such extremes that he had to flee town — the alternative would have been severe punishment by the enraged parishioners.

The church building of 1752 might have been replaced by another log church, or the original might have withstood the flood of 1785 to be moved to the site of the present church, facing the town square, in the 1790s. A visitor described it shortly after it was placed at the new site:

> At the upper end there is a beautiful altar, the fronton of which is brass gilt and enriched in medio-relievo representing the religious of the world, diffusing the benefits of the gospel over the new world. In the middle of the altar there is a crucifix of brass gilt and underneath a copy of a picture by Raphael, representing the Madonna and Child, St. Elizabeth and St. John. In the second group there is a St. Joseph, all

perfectly well drawn and colored. The beauty and grace of the Virgin are beyond description and the little Jesus and St. John are charming.

This church was replaced in 1835 by a stone church of proportions considered huge by the standards of the time.

Except for the vaulting and the roof, the present great church was designed by the legendary Francis Xavier Weiss, pastor of the parish of Ste. Geneviève from 1865 to 1900. The cornerstone was laid on April 30, 1876, and the building was consecrated on September 29, 1880. Three-fourths of the cost of the church was donated by Odile Pratte Vallé, widow of Felix Vallé, a grandson of old François Vallé I.

While times in the Middle Valley were peaceful and wholesome, such was not the case in Europe. Royalty, resentful of papal aspirations to political power and recognizing the great value of the support given to the Vatican by the Society of Jesus, decided to blow the whistle. Orders were issued suppressing the Jesuits in France, and recalling all those in service in the New World. They were commanded to proceed immediately to New Orleans for transportation back to France. Their possessions were seized, sold to the highest bidders, and the proceeds applied against their transportation costs. Eleven years later, Pope Clement XIV suppressed the order throughout the world.

Thus, the force which inspired exploration, and established and sustained a high order of civilization on both sides of the Mississippi River, was removed by an act 5,000 miles away.

The embittered Jesuits left. In all the Middle Valley there was but one priest — the Franciscan Luc Collet, hiding from the British near Cahokia.

One Jesuit, Sebastian Meurin, was so devoted to the people of Ste. Genevieve that he approached the superior council in New Orleans and asked them to allow him to return to the Middle Valley. They acceded to this request, with the proviso that Meurin was to "recognize no other ecclesiastical superior than the reverend Father Superior of the Capuchins at New Orleans." (Both Quebec and New Orleans at that time were claiming jurisdiction over the Middle Valley.)

So Meurin returned, alone, back up the broad river to Ste. Genevieve. Back to the perils of ministering to an area of thousands of square miles by canoe and horseback. He had been home only a few weeks when he was called upon to administer a baptism in the town of St. Louis, then only two months old, and that entry is the first in the ancient records of the Old Cathedral on the downtown St. Louis riverfront.

Meurin spent most of the years following his return rushing from one settlement to another for baptisms, weddings, last rites, and burials. The strain was so great that he appealed for help wherever he could. Disregarding orders, he wrote to Quebec. Bishop Briand, so moved by Meurin's plea, advised the beleaguered cleric that he not only would send help, but he would appoint Meurin vicar general over the entire Illinois country, including New Orleans. Philippe François de Rastal, Chevalier de Rocheblave and Spanish commandant at Ste. Genevieve, put a price on Meurin's head, but the devoted people of Ste. Genevieve were able to warn their priest in time. In 1768 he went into hiding along the west bank, traveling to the settlements between Ste. Genevieve and St. Louis in the dead of night.

During the succeeding years the kindly Meurin watched the Mississippi enroaching on the graveyard near old Fort de Chartres and moved the bodies of Collet and Gagnon to Prairie du Rocher.

Briand was a man of his word. Within months after receipt of Meurin's appeal he sent the thirty-one-year-old Pierre Gibault to help the sixty-one-year-old Jesuit.

Gibault was at home in the wilderness, and he covered the area with speed and enthusiasm, roaming as far to the east as Post Vincennes, making friends and converts wherever he went. Not long after his arrival on June 24, 1770, he was called upon to bless the first church in St. Louis.

The jockeying for power in the Europe of the 1760s and the French and Indian War in North America had drastic effects upon the peaceful population of the Middle Valley. The Treaty of Paris, enacted in 1763 at the close of the Seven Years' War, forced France to cede to England all lands east of the Mississippi River, resulting in grave discontent among the occupants of the east bank.

Scores of inhabitants abandoned their homes in Kaskaskia to live in Ste. Genevieve, rather than offer their allegiance to the despised George III. Young Auguste Chouteau capitalized upon this near panic by persuading many of the occupants of the settlements north of Kaskaskia to move to St. Louis rather than make the arduous trek downstream to New Orleans, where the Spanish still reigned. There was still some apprehension on the part of the migrants to the west bank when it was learned that the Secret Treaty of Fontainebleau, proclaimed in April 1764, removed their new home from the aegis of the Bourbon kings and placed them under the Spanish crown. But any government was better than British government.

Thus, it comes as no surprise that the French of the area, like their brothers on the continent, sided with the colonists in the American Revolutionary War. The crude, raucous, and often lawless Americans would make better neighbors than the English.

Still, the French delivered only passive support — until the quiet of the night of July 4, 1778, was broken by the triumphant hoots of a company of Kentucky woodsmen under the leadership of the Virginian, George Rogers Clark. They came to Kaskaskia that night, flying the colors of the Commonwealth of Virginia. While the victory-flushed Long Knives knew they outnumbered the small British garrison, they were equally aware that the townspeople greatly outnumbered them. They needed politics to beef up their muskets. They needed Gibault.

Gibault and Clark met that night to discuss the terms of the surrender of the town. The priest entered the narthex of his church and tolled its bell, summoning the townspeople to a meeting. Gibault assured the parishioners that they would be wise in following their sentiments in acquiescence to the American demands, a recommendation which the townspeople readily accepted. The flag of Virginia was raised without the firing of a single shot.

Clark was far from through with Gibault. He persuaded the priest to accompany a detachment through the forests to Post Vincennes, 145 miles due east. There the British garrison would be ready and waiting — the Long Knives would need all the persuasion Gibault could deliver for them.

Yet, Gibault, with Clark and Dr. Jean-Baptiste Laffont of Kaskaskia, needed only two days to bring the people and garrison at Vincennes to the side of the Americans.

The vain Clark, who wrote with disdain of Gibault's role, nevertheless regarded the priest's political prowess highly. When the commandant of the British garrison at Detroit put a price on Gibault's head, Clark lost no time in spiriting him into hiding.

It was left to the celebrated Patrick Henry to correctly appraise Gibault's role in the Middle Valley campaign: "This country owes many thing to Gibault, for his zeal and services."

Having been transferred to Kaskaskia from Ste. Genevieve in 1773, Gibault was reappointed pastor of Ste. Genevieve in 1778, where he served until 1784. He was a familiar sight to settlers for miles around — a small man on a great horse, carrying the sacred accouterments of his office in his saddlebags and a rifle across the saddle bow. In his belt were a brace of pistols and a wicked-looking knife. Gibault, the man of God, was willing to trust his survival to the Almighty, with perhaps a bit of help from his belt. He was sent to New Madrid in July, 1793, where he remained until his death on August 16, 1802. For thirty-four years he had served his fellow men. After the death of the aged Meurin in 1777 Gibault served the entire area alone, as Meurin had done before him.

Few historians would argue that this pioneer priest was a valuable ally to the cause of the American Revolution, for he delivered virtually all of what is now southern Illinois to the Americans, providing an effective barrier along the great waterway which would have linked the British garrisons in the north to the Gulf of Mexico. Yet, Gibault is virtually unknown today.

CHAPTER VII.

From France to Spain to the U.S.A.

His given name was François but hardly anyone in the little village of Ste. Genevieve knew the man by any name but Papa Vallé. The name Vallé still is heard in Ste. Genevieve. The earlist Vallé, Pierre, emigrated from Rouen, Normandy, to Quebec in 1645. His son Charles married a Genevieve Marcou(x) and one of their sons was François Vallé — the beloved Papa Vallé of Ste. Genevieve. He was born January 2, 1716.

He moved to Kaskaskia in 1740, and in that year married Marianne Billeron. Soon after, the couple moved to Ste. Genevieve, where all their children were born. There were sons François, Jr., Jean Baptiste, Charles, Joseph, and two daughters, Marie and Marguerite.

The family prospered — fifteen years after their arrival in Ste. Genevieve the Vallé family was known to be the wealthiest in the Middle Valley. Philip Pittman, writing after 1764, said: "Vallé was the richest inhabitant of the country of the Illinois; he raised great quantities of corn and provisions; was the owner of 100 slaves, and in addition hired white people and kept them constantly employed.''

Papa Vallé was an astute man too. Having lived under the lilies of France all his life, he couldn't have welcomed the news of the transfer of western Louisiana to Spain. Yet, when Don Pedro Piernas passed through Ste. Genevieve en route to his headquarters in St. Louis he was welcomed by Papa Vallé like an old friend. This, despite the fact Vallé's friends and associates had urged him to take them elsewhere, away from direct Spanish rule.

Piernas came to Ste. Genevieve with his tired and hungry detachment of troops. Papa Vallé fed them. It developed that Don Pedro was as short of cash as he was of food. Papa Vallé loaned him money.

His reward was not long in coming. The gratitude of Piernas was such that he appointed Papa Vallé both civil and military commandant of Ste. Genevieve. As such he became commanding officer of one lieutenant, one corporal, and seven soldiers. (The officers and each of the men received two pair of shoes, two pairs of stockings, two shirts, and one new suit annually.)

Later the garrison was changed to include Vallé; Don F. Charpentier, lieutenant; Don F. Du Chouquette as sub-lieutenant; plus a first sergeant, two second sergeants, four first corporals, four second corporals, and all citizens between fifteen and fifty years of age who were capable of bearing arms.

François Vallé was not a man given to temper. Even during the trying months when his oldest son was infatuated with a beautiful mulatto woman from the village, the patriarch kept his tongue while the affair ran its course. There is but one recorded instance when he abandoned his aplomb. A resident named Pierre Masse, known as Picard, disputed his word concerning a payment for a quantity of lead. Vallé picked Picard up bodily and smashed him against a trunk, threatening him with imprisonment if he didn't pay his bill. Since he was directly involved, Vallé reported the incident to Don Francisco Cruzat, the successor to Piernas, for judgment. Vallé's tormentor was sentenced to make a public apology and serve seven days in jail.

The Ste. Genevieve jail was, of course, under the direct jurisdiction of Papa Vallé. Such was his nature that when some unfortunate soul was forced to lodge there Papa Vallé would send down some whiskey "to blunt the acuteness of his feelings and to render the reflections of his first hours as little bitter as possible."

One can't help but wonder if Picard ever got his booze.

Like most of the French, Vallé was a strong supporter of the American cause during the Revolution. He was often called upon to house American troops and he furnished liberal stores to Indians pressed into garrisons. He dispatched a contingent of Indians under his jurisdiction to the defense of Fort Jefferson.

Papa Vallé died in 1783, having served for nineteen years as both civil and military commandant of Ste. Genevieve. At the age of sixty-seven, he was laid to rest in the alluvium of *le grand champ*. His grave marker probably was washed away within a few years. His bones probably are still there.

Vallé was succeeded as military commandant by Don Sylvio Francisco de Cartabona, who arrived in Ste. Genevieve in 1784. It was Cartabona who took over the defense of St. Louis in 1780, shortly after the death of Don Fernando DeLeyba, who was commandant there at the time of the Indian attack.

In April 1787 he was succeeded in Ste. Geneviève by Henri Peyroux de la Coudrenière, an infantry captain and respected author of several geographical publications.

Nine years later Peyroux was replaced by François Vallé, Jr., thirty-eight-year-old son of the original commandant. The younger Vallé was married to Marie Carpentier and the two lived in a one-story frame building with wide galleries on the bank of South Gabouri Creek.

(This is the house that has fooled more than one historian into thinking it no longer exists. It does exist, but it was stripped of its galleries and great Norman truss possibly a century ago.)

Joseph Coulture, who had been flooded out countless times, had had enough of the Mississippi by 1778. That year he moved his family and his possessions to the high ground between the two forks of the Gabouri — thus becoming the first settler of record on *les petite côtes.*

Young Vallé is supposed to have been one of the early builders in the new village upstream from *le grand champ* — a distinct possibility since after his father's passing he probably had the capital and the manpower to accomplish the job. The house was supposed to have been built on that site, not moved. It probably was built in 1791.

Others of the first settlers in the new town were Jacques Boyer, M. Loisette, J. B. La Croise, Sr., J. B. and Vital Beauvais (known as St. Jeme or St. Gemme) and J. B. Sebastian Pratte. François Janis moved over from Kaskaskia in 1790, along with Parfait Dufour.

Many other east bank pioneers, full of loathing for

the uncouth American invaders, came to Ste. Genevieve — from Kaskaskia, Prairie du Rocher, even Cahokia. (Spanish authorities were under orders to refuse to issue passports to emigrants who did not profess the Catholic faith — an edict which served to bar most Americans from settlement on the west bank. The authorities in St. Louis winked at this law. There is no evidence to indicate that it was ignored in Ste. Genevieve.)

The old townsite was virtually abandoned by 1791 except for a building or two. The church was moved up in 1794.

Vallé left other structural legacies. There no longer is any trace of the mill he built on Dodge Creek in 1793, or of the water-powered sawmill on the *Aux Vases*. But the great mill on the bank of the Saline, where the old lead road fords, still stands. It was gutted by a fire in 1864, sixty-four years after it was built, but its towering, groteque limestone walls still rise sixty-five feet above the stream. The ruin is only fifteen yards away from the bank but the foliage is so dense that the structure is nearly invisible from the bridge, no more than 100 yards downstream.

It is possible that the stone for this building came from the ruins of old Fort de Chartres. Much of the fort's rock is believed to have been incorporated into the construction of some of the early Ste. Genevieve homes.

François Vallé, Jr., died on March 6, 1804, just four days before consummation of the Louisiana Purchase. He was buried beneath his pew near the communion rail of the old log church. The grave was moved during the construction of the rock church in 1834, and again during the building of the present structure. It is marked today by a bronze plaque imbedded in the floor.

On March 10, 1804, Israel Dodge, father, grandfather, and stepfather of future United States senators, quietly raised the American flag above the mourning town — mourning the death of its first citizen, the death of an era, the death of an empire. For that was the end of France in North America.

CHAPTER VIII.

An Unfortunate Fort

François Vallé II was succeeded as civil commandant by his only surviving brother, Jean Baptiste
Vallé. J. B. Vallé was a prosperous merchant, a
sometime mountain man, and a partner in the fur
trading venture known as Menard and Vallé. His
home was one of the first built in the new town.

He was married to Jeanne Barbeau, daughter of the
French army engineer who constructed Fort de
Chartres. By the time he was twenty-seven (in 1787) he
had two children, thirty-seven slaves, and the finest
home in town. Upon the tranfer of Louisiana to the
United States, Territorial Governor William Henry
Harrison appointed Vallé civil commandant, and he is
said to have exercised the judicial powers of this office
for the rest of his long life.

One old settler, writing a century ago, recalled that
even in his last years Vallé wore the cocked hat, knee
breeches and broad-cuffed coat of the eighteenth
century, a living memorial to a dead regime.

His home, which still stands on the northwest corner
of Main and Market streets in Ste. Genevieve, is
surrounded with mystery.

The biggest puzzle is in the basement. There the walls are far thicker (three to four feet) than necessary to support the superstructure. The rumor persists that this portion of the structure was used as a fort, built perhaps as early as 1762. The foundation wall indeed has this appearance — the corners bulge with massive three-quarter-round emplacements, possibly intended as tower foundations. Even the loopholes remain. Yet, there is no authoritative documentation to suggest this was ever used as a fort. It is, after all, underground; it is possible that earth fill could have been used to bring the house lot high enough to avoid the floods.

Even the builder of the house remains a mystery. Some texts credit it to J. B. Vallé, but some others say that François Vallé II erected the building.

There is a possibility that François Vallé II, after erecting the family place on the South Gabouri, immediately started construction of a fortification at Main and Market, 450 feet to the north. Upon the death of François II at the age of forty-six, it could be presumed that J. B. Vallé completed the construction, but as a residence rather than as a fort.

The existence of a fort at all in the old town has also been somewhat of a mystery. The Catholic archives vaguely refer to the presence of one on *le grand champ* in 1759. In all probability, the term garrison house should have been used, although it was referred to as Fort Joachim.

There definitely was a fort on the bank of the South Gabouri, possibly erected before the year of the great flood. A plate in Father Yealy's book places it very close to the François Vallé house, based upon the survey of 1817. Gen. Victor Collot wrote that he had seen that fort on the bank in 1790. He described it as being too far from the Mississippi and extremely vulnerable to an attack from the high ground behind it. General Collot observed that the fort was comparable to, but smaller than, the fort in St. Louis. This would mean it had circular stone towers placed at intervals, connected with a wood stockade. The J. B. Vallé house foundation certainly doesn't fit such a description.

The files of the Ste. Genevieve *Fair Play* contain an account of an interview with Celeste Thomure in 1888, in which she states that the François Vallé house itself served as the fort. The woman was ninety years old at the time, however, and recollections of events long past often are inaccurate.

The noted architectural historian Charles E. Peterson wrote that the fort was in existence in 1796 — small, square and surrounded with pickets. He stated that it was armed with two, two-pound cannons and manned by a corporal and two men.

An old map recently found identifies an old fort on the northwest corner of South Gabouri and Main streets. Street repair crewmen found evidence of pickets in the soil when they excavated for street widening in the 1960s.

It remained for Carl J. Ekberg to answer most of the questions about Ste. Genevieve's old fort. Built under the direction of the St. Louis surveyor, Antoine Soulard, it was a wood palisaded structure, about 192 feet square, with a bastion in each corner. It was financed personally by François Vallé, who was later reimbursed by the crown for its cost. It was erected in 1794 on the hill, now gone, immediately south of the South Gabouri; but the precise location is still a mystery and shall remain so until an archaeological study can be made.

CHAPTER IX.

Indians — Friends and Enemies

The absence of class consciousness among the Ste. Genevieve French soon eliminated any hostility the Indians might have held for them. Since the Indian usually was not held as personal property, as was the black slave, there was little opportunity for close personal communion. There were some Indian slaves at first, but the practice soon became taboo in the colonial community. The red man preferred to live in his own villages. There was social intercourse of considerable consequence, plus a great deal of commercial traffic.

A village of Peorias and Kickapoos was located on *le grand champ,* close enough to be a suburb of Ste. Genevieve. The red and white children played side by side in the narrow streets.

While the Peorias enjoyed peaceful relations with the Ste. Genevieve residents, they were subject to almost constant harassment from other tribes. One of their number murdered the Ottawa chief, Pontiac, in Cahokia in 1769, and subsequent acts of retribution drove them to the Ste. Genevieve area in 1780. The distance decreased the trouble but didn't eliminate it.

The Peorias were able to save two or three bushels of corn and beans a year, plus dried pumpkins and dried meat. After their fall hunt they stayed in their villages until February or March, when they went on another hunt. Their crops were planted in April and the summer hunt took place in May. They often supplemented their diet with berries and nuts.

A village of Shawnees settled near Apple Creek, forty-five miles downstream, in 1800. They patterned their vertical log houses after those of the Ste. Genevieve settlers.

The Kaskaskias eventually migrated west and now are located in northeastern Oklahoma. By 1945 remnants of the once-great Illinois confederation numbered only 413 persons.

The only Indians truly native to Missouri were the Missouris and the Osage. The Missouris spoke the Chiwere Sioux language. They built lodges of poles covered with mats. The Osage also spoke a Siouan dialect. They had no permanent villages near Ste. Genevieve, although they certainly made themselves at home in the area. Most of their villages were in western Missouri and consisted of a complex of rectangular houses. Ranging from thirty-one to forty-two feet long and from fifteen to twenty-two feet wide, they were supported by center posts joined with ridge poles. Bent poles formed the roof.

The Delawares and Shawnees were moved into the area by the Spanish in 1789. They were repeatedly called upon to raid the meandering Osage groups.

Throughout the Spanish regime the settlers were troubled by the Osage. While the Osage were reluctant to kill, they would steal with brazen impunity, often subjecting their victims to gross indignites in the process. Ste. Genevieve, of all the settlements along the Mississippi, seemed to be the center of their activities, probably because of the pacific attitudes of its populace. The muscular Osage warriors, few of them less than six feet tall, would enter the town during the night, divide into small parties and carry off anything they could find. They broke into stables and led the livestock away. Then they would unite a short distance from the town and march leisurely away, driving their horses ahead of them, with no fear of being pursued.

In the forest or on the plains they were kings. The little encampment of Peorias and Kickapoos on *le grand champ* eventually was forced to curtail their hunts, such was their fear of the Osage.

A group of seven men working the lead vein at Mine La Motte on April 7, 1774, was murdered by a band of Osage. Included was young Joseph Vallé, twenty-year-old son of Papa Vallé.

There is a report of a man named Henry Fry, who left Big River with his fiancee, her brother, and two sisters, bound for Ste. Genevieve and marriage. In the vicinity of Terre Blue Creek, some nine miles north of Farmington, they were overtaken by a band of sixty Osage and robbed of their horses, guns, and furs worth $1,500. They stripped Fry and ordered him to run. When he refused they beat him with their ramrods and stripped all the others except the bride's brother. One of her sisters was dragged naked through a field of burnt stubble. Her brother, Aaron Baker, having a fortuitous case of acne, was thought by the Osage to have smallpox and was left alone.

It wasn't until after the immigration of the

Americans, who regarded shooting Indians as being somewhat akin to squirrel hunting, that the Osage met their match and retreated to western Missouri.

CHAPTER X.

Lead, Commerce, and Birdwatching

The people of Ste. Genevieve (and all historians interested in that area, for that matter) are immensely indebted to Henry Marie Brackenridge. At the age of seven he was sent alone down the Ohio from Pittsburgh in the early 1790s by his father, Judge H. H. Brackenridge. He left a graphic account of his life in Ste. Genevieve with the family of Vital St. Gemme Beauvais. The house where he lived still is standing, although substantially altered. Unlike the accounts of so many other observers, his recollections ring true with the evidence. The purpose of his visit, evidently, was to learn the language of the French.

Of the Beauvais family, he had this to say:

> M. Beauvais was a tall, dry, old French Canadian, dressed in the costume of the place; that is, with a blue cotton handkerchief on his head, one corner thereof descending behind and partly covering the eel-skin which bound his hair, a check shirt, coarse linen pantaloons on his hips, and the Indian sandal or moccasin, the only covering to the feet worn here by both sexes. He was a man of grave and serious aspect, entirely

unlike the gay Frenchman we are accustomed to see; and this seriousness was not a little heightened by the fixed rigidity of the maxillary muscles, occasioned by having his pipe continually in his mouth, except while in bed, or at Mass, or during meals. Let it not be supposed that I mean to speak disrespectfully or with levity, of a most estimable man; my object in describing him is to give an idea of many other fathers of families of the village. Madame Beauvais was a large fat lady, with an open cheerful countenance, and an expression of kindness and affection to her numerous offspring, and to all others excepting her colored domestics, toward whom she was rigid and severe. She was, notwithstanding, a most pious and excellent woman, and, as a French wife ought to be, completely mistress of the family.

Brackenridge observed that when he arrived in Ste. Genevieve not a soul knew a word of English, and he knew but two words of French. His contemporaries, however, did not ridicule his handicap, but seemed to take pleasure in helping him learn their language.

Madame Beauvais took her religion seriously — she refused to put the Brackenridge boy to bed with her own children until he had been baptised.

He leaves an account of what appears to be the first school in Ste. Genevieve. It evidently was established prior to 1795, for in that year Pierre Charles Peyroux gave it land and something of a library. The teacher was reported to be François Moreaux, whose descendants still live in the old town. (That is improbable, as he couldn't sign his own marriage contract.) The school evidently ceased operation after only a few years.

Brackenridge described the Beauvais property:

. . . a long, low building, with a porch or shed in front and another in the rear; the chimney occupied the center, dividing the house into two parts, with each a fireplace. One of these parts served for dining-room, parlor, and principal bed-chamber; the other was the kitchen; and each had a small room taken off at the end for private chambers or cabinets. There was no loft or garret, a pair of stairs being a rare thing in the village. The furniture, excepting the beds and the looking glass, was of the most common kind, consisting of an armoire, a rough table or two, and some coarse chairs. The yard was enclosed with cedar pickets, eight or ten inches in diameter and seven feet high, placed upright, sharpened at the top, in the manner of a stockade fort. In front the yard was narrow, but in the rear quite spacious, and containing the barn and stables, the negro quarters, and all the necessary offices of a farm-yard. Beyond this there was a spacious garden enclosed with pickets in the same manner as the yard. It was, indeed, a garden — in which the greatest variety and the finest vegetables were cultivated, intermingled with flowers and shrubs; on one side of it there was a small orchard containing a variety of the choicest fruits. The subsantial and permanent character of these enclosures is in singular contrast with the slight and temporary fences and palings of the Americans. The house was a ponderous wooden frame, which, instead of being weather-boarded, was filled in with clay, and then whitewashed. As to the living, the table was provided in a very different manner from that of the generality of Americans. With the poorest French peasant, cookery is an art well understood. They make great use of vegetables, and prepared in a manner to be wholesome and palatable.

The description Brackenridge leaves of the Sunday balls is somewhat different from the accounts of others. Possibly this is because the balls the children attended were quite different from those patronized exclusively by adults.

> I sometimes went with other children to the ball, which was by no means a place of frivolity, but rather a school of manners. The children of the rich and poor were placed on a footing of perfect equality and the only difference was a more costly, but not a cleaner or neater dress. The strictest decorum and propriety were preserved by the parents who were present. There was as much solemnity and seriousness at these assemblies as at our Sunday schools; the children were required to be seated, and no confusion or disorder was permitted. The minuet was the principal dance. I think it is in some measure owing to this practice that the awkward, clownish manners of other nations are scarcely known among the French. The secret of true politeness, self-denial, or the giving the better place to others, was taught me at these little balls.

Within a few decades of the founding of Ste. Genevieve, mining had joined agriculture as a leading producer of revenue.

At the turn of the century lead was important in Ste. Genevieve. Many habitations had some sort of space reserved for the storage of lead. In 1778 Vital St. Gemme Beauvais and François Vallé I made a general claim of sixty feet around every hill in the area that might contain minerals.

Mine la Motte, supposedly founded by LaMothe de

Cadillac, was located near the head of the St. Francis River, Mine à Joe near the present town of Flat River, Mine à Burton on a branch of the Mineral Fork, Old Mines near the town of the same name, and Renault's Mines on the Mineral Fork and the Fourche Arno. By 1804 there were ten working lead mines in the area, and by 1817 production was up to 800,000 pounds annually.

Henry Rowe Schoolcraft, in a book published in 1819, described a personal encounter with a man he identified as a Mr. Burton, an aged miner. This actually was François Azor, a native of Brittany, who was referred to as the Breton, a name the Americans corrupted to Burton. Azor supposedly was born in 1710. In 1818, at the age of 108, he was still going strong, walking the two miles from his home to the church for Mass every Sunday.

While hunting in the area southeast of Mine Renault in 1773, Azor stumbled across a rich deposit of lead which came to be known as Mine à Burton. It is located near Potosi.

Schoolcraft said that miners were paid four cents a pound for lead at the big warehouses which had been erected at the Ste. Genevieve landing.

The lead was treated in various ways at the mines. It was soaked in vinegar to obtain white lead, used in the manufacture of paint. It was heated, sifted, and reheated to make red lead.

Towers built in nearby Herculaneum were used in the manufacture of shot. The molten lead dripped through a copper sieve, then fell into a cistern below. The largest shot was dropped from a height of 140 feet; smaller pellets fell about ninety feet. The shot then was cranked in cylindrical vessels for roundness. Plumbago (graphite) was added for gloss. Each man was capable of producing 4,000 pounds of shot a day.

It might be said that the state of Texas was founded from Ste. Genevieve, because one of the residents of the community was Moses Austin, who, with his son Stephen, looms large in Texas history.

Born in Durham, Connecticut, in 1764, Moses Austin moved to Philadelphia as a young man, where be became a merchant. He took over a pewter button factory in Richmond, Virginia, where he operated a country store and a small lead mine.

In the fall of 1796 he came to St. Louis, then moved to Ste. Genevieve, where he took over the operation of Mine á Burton in 1798. He brought his family, including Stephen, then five, to Ste. Genevieve in 1798, the same year he received a nine-square-mile land grant in the Potosi area. Records indicate he settled his family in a large house, probably located on the triangular plot between the Ratte-Hoffman house and the South Gabouri, a few yards east of the old St. Marys Road.

Austin, a resourceful miner, erected the area's first reverbatory furnace. He turned out nearly 300 tons of lead a year, building a substantial fortune from his sheet lead and shot production. His success was such that he was able to erect a sawmill and a grist mill in in 1799 and then a palatial residence, "Durham Hall," which became the nucleus of the American settlement west of Ste. Genevieve. He and his fifty employees survived violent Osage attacks in 1799 and 1802, largely because of the persuasive powers of a three-pounder imported for such occasions.

The failure of a St. Louis bank during the panic of 1818 wiped Austin out, but he had had enough prosperity anyway. He decided to form a colony in Texas. He died in 1821 while on a return trip to Ste. Genevieve and is interred in the Presbyterian cemetery at Potosi. Attempts by the state of Texas to move his body to Austin have so far been fruitless.

Probably the most noted person ever to settle in Ste. Genevieve, albeit briefly, was the celebrated ornthologist, John James Audubon. He came not as a birdwatcher, but as a businessman. He left as a birdwatcher, though.

Audubon, born in the West Indies in 1780, was taken by his family to France while an infant. While in his twenties be became acquainted with young Ferdinand Rozier, a native of Nantes. Both of them served in the Napoleonic navy.

Despite his obvious talents as an artist and lover of nature, Audubon was determined to be a man of commerce. He saw in Rozier much of this same determination, and the two elected to abandon the devastated homeland and pursue their careers in America.

They arrived in New York May 26, 1806, and settled in Pennsylvania for a year. Then they loaded a keelboat with merchandise and headed for Kentucky, where they engaged in retail trade for three years.

In the fall of 1810 Audubon and Rozier loaded another keelboat with 300 barrels of whiskey and other goods and set out for Ste. Genevieve. An account of their trip, quoted from Audubon, is left by Rozier's son, Gen. Firmin A Rozier:

> After floating down the Ohio, we entered the Mississippi River running three miles an hour, and bringing shoals of ice to further impede our progress.

The patron ordered the line ashore, and it became the duty of every man "to haul the cordelle," which was a rope fastened to the bow of the boat, and one man left on board to steer, the others laying the rope over their shoulders, slowly wafted the heavy boat and cargo against the current. We made seven miles that day . . . At night we camped on the shores. Here we made fires, cooked supper, and setting one sentinel, the rest went to bed. . . .

[Three] more days of similar toil followed, when the weather became severe, and our patron ordered us to go into winter quarters, in the great bend of the Tawapattee Bottom.

There was not a white man's cabin within twenty miles, and that over a river we could not cross. We cut down trees and made a winter camp . . . I rambled through the deep forests, and soon became acquainted with the Indian trails and the lakes in the neighborhood.

. . . I was not long in meeting strolling natives in the woods. They gradually accumulated, and before a week had passed, great numbers of these unfortunate beings were around us, chiefly Osages and Shawnees.

. . . Here I passed six weeks pleasantly, investigating the habits of wild deer, bears, cougars, raccoons and turkeys, and many other animals, and I drew more or less by the side of our great camp-fire every day . . . What a good fire it is . . . Imagine four or five ash trees, three feet in diameter and sixty feet long cut piled up, with all their limbs and branches, ten feet high, and then a fire kindled on the top with brush and dry leaves; and then under the smoke the party lies down and goes to sleep.

While our time went pleasantly enough, a sudden and startling catastrophy threatened us without warning. The ice began to break, and our boat was in danger of being cut to pieces by the ice-floes, or swamped by their pressure. [The ice] split with reports like those of heavy artillery.

While we were gazing on this scene, a tremendous crash was heard, when suddenly the great dam of ice gave way, and in less than four hours, we witnessed the complete breaking up of the ice. The cargo was again put on board . . . and our camp given up to the Indians. After bidding mutual adieus . . . fortunately we reached safely Cape Girardeau. But this village was small, and no market for us, and we determined to push up to Ste. Genevieve.

We arrived in a few days at the Grand Tower Missouri, where an immense rock in the stream makes navigation dangerous. Here we used out cordelles, and with great difficulty and peril passed it safely . . . We arrived at Ste. Genevieve and found a favorable market.

While the market may have proved favorable to Audubon, Audubon did not exactly prove favorable to Rozier. Both were gentle men, but the Pennsylvania and the Kentucky experiences proved that the partnership was unfair to Rozier. They parted company only a few weeks after their arrival in Ste. Genevieve. Audubon dispensed with the tiny cabin he had built on the site of the town's first bank and headed back to Kentucky. He engaged in a milling venture there which soon went down. Audubon was literally forced to pursue ornithology as a career.

Rozier remained, and so intense was his impact on the community that to this day both a department store and a bank bear his name. His descendants still live in the old homes. He married Constance Roy in 1813 and the couple had ten children. He died in 1864 at the age of eighty-six.

Lead may have been important to all Ste. Genevieve commerce, but other forms of commercial endeavor should be recognized. One of the most colorful pieces of Americana was the general store, and Ste. Genevieve had some dandies. An old account book in the archives of the Missouri Historical Society listed some of the goods and services vended in one such store: groceries, meats, dry goods, hardware, shoes, stationery, glasses, toothbrushes, fiddle strings, and real estate. The store also served as the business agent of what amounted to a musician's union.

The bills were paid in lead, salt, and pelts. Sometimes they were paid by check.

Due to the proximity of Saline Creek there was always salt. It brought about $2 for a sixty-pound bushel.

In 1796 the industry in Ste. Genevieve proper was limited to two water mills, a horse mill, and a pottery kiln. The first stream mill was built by Edward Walsh in 1818, and Schoolcraft observed two brickyards there in 1819. He also commented on the abundance of siliceous sand "in the interior, which I think adapted for the manufacture of flint glass." The site is near Potosi. Ste. Genevieve missed out on that one though. The sugar-like sand indeed was ideal for glass making purposes, but the townspeople weren't particularly receptive to the suggestions that the Pittsburgh Plate Glass Company erect a plant there. The installation went to Crystal City, about thirty miles northwest. For some unknown reason the city fathers also turned down the opportunity to have Southeast Missouri State College located there — it went to Cape Girardeau instead.

More industry probably would have located in Ste. Genevieve in the early days but the old town probably was plagued with a shortage of available work force. This problem was intensified to some degree by the adoption programs of some large cities. Local citizens could petition for an orphan, who would agree to work without pay if the citizen would provide decent food, clothing, shelter, and the opportunity to learn a trade At the age of twenty-one the orphan was set free from obligation and often chose to settle in the city rather than return to the rural area.

CHAPTER XI.

Ste. Genevieve Loads the U.S. Senate

If Virginia is the cradle of presidents, Ste. Genevieve must be the cradle of United States senators — no fewer than five of them had their roots in the old town. Towering above them all was Dr. Lewis F. Linn, the man whose advocacy of the prompt settlement of the Pacific Northwest secured the American claim against Britain for sovereignty over Oregon and Washington.

Old Israel Dodge had something in common with three of those senators. He had moved from present-day Kansas in the 1790s to a farm on Saline Creek. He operated the ancient salt works there around 1800 and built a fine home in the area in 1805, the year he was elected the first sheriff of the Ste. Genevieve District. His son was Henry Dodge, who was to become one of the two first senators from the new state of Wisconsin.

Henry Dodge was born in 1782 in Vincennes, Indiana. After moving to Ste. Genevieve he helped his father operate the salt works, then succeeded him as sheriff. He later was appointed a United States marshal for the territory of Missouri. He was governor of the Wisconsin Territory from 1836 to 1841, by appointment of President Andrew Jackson. At the time the territory included the present state of Wisconsin, the Dakotas, Iowa, and Minnesota. Then he became a delegate to Congress from that area and again occupied the statehouse from 1845 until 1848.

Dodge was elected to the Senate upon admission of Wisconsin to the Union in 1848, where he served until 1857. He died ten years later.

Henry Dodge's son, Augustus C. Dodge, who was born in Ste. Genevieve in 1812, became one of the first two senators from Iowa. He married a Ste. Genevieve woman, Clara Hertick, and moved to the Wisconsin Territory when he was twenty-seven. After fighting in both the Black Hawk and the Winnebago wars he served as a delegate to Congress from 1841 to 1847. He was a senator from 1848 to 1855, after which he was named U.S. minister of the court of Madrid. He died in Burlington in 1883.

Dr. Linn is referred to in a number of documents as the half-brother of Henry Dodge, which probably is true. One source (Rozier) identifies Linn's mother as the widow of Israel Dodge, but this is most unlikely. Dodge and Linn's mother were probably divorced.

Linn was born in Louisville in 1795. Upon the death of his parents, Henry Dodge assumed guardianship, including the burden of Linn's education in a Louisville medical school. Linn spent the years from 1815 to 1830 in Ste. Genevieve. After serving for three years as a state senator he was appointed to fill the unexpired term of U.S. Senator Alexander Buckner in 1833.

Linn had become quite learned in the treatment and causes of cholera, assembling a fund of information from doctors and hospitals in European and eastern U.S. cities which had been ravaged by the disease. At one time he left his duties at the capitol to return to Ste. Genevieve and help arrest an outbreak of cholera, only to acquire the disease himself in the process. He died in office in 1843.

Linn's epitaph in the Protestant section of the old cemetery describes him as the "Model Senator from Missouri," a claim which seems to have some basis in fact. Rozier's book contains an undocumented tale of Linn's popularity among his colleagues in the Senate:

> One one occasion, when he held in his hands a roll of bills to present, and had risen for that purpose, Mr. [James] Buchanan rose and remarked pleasantly, "Doctor, we will save you trouble if you recommend them; we will pass the whole bundle." The suggestion was, in the same spirit, seconded by Mr. [Henry] Clay. On another occasion, whilst a debate ran high, the Senators being excited on some political question, Henry Clay made a statement which caused Senator Linn to rise to correct him. Immediately Clay paused and bowed, and waving gracefully his hand, repiled, "It is sufficient that it come from the Senator from Missouri."

That quote might seem questionable to those familiar with the pyrotechnics on the floor of the contemporary Senate. This feeling is enhanced by the knowledge that General Rozier was seventy when he wrote the preceeding lines about incidents which allegedly occurred a half-century earlier. Clay could be a holy terror on the Senate floor. Either he wanted to concede the point or he owed Linn a whopper of a doctor's bill.

It is a surprising coincidence that both the initial

senators from the new state of Iowa were from Ste.
Genevieve. George W. Jones joined Augustus Dodge
in 1848 and served two terms. The son of Judge John
Rice Jones, he was born in Vincennes in 1804. The
family came to Ste. Genevieve five years later. George
Jones married a Ste. Genevieve woman, Josephine
Gregoire, then studied law at Lexington, Kentucky.
They moved to Iowa in 1827, and he was appointed
postmaster in a little town near Dubuque in 1833. Two
years later he was appointed a delegate to Congress,
where he served until 1841. Following his terms in
Washington he was named U.S. minister to Columbia. He died in Dubuque in 1896.

Lewis V. Bogy, the only one of the five senators who
was born in Ste. Genevieve, studied law at Lexington
under Nathaniel Pope. In 1832, at the age of nineteen,
he served in the Black Hawk War. He returned to Ste.
Genevieve in 1835, moved shortly thereafter to St.
Louis, and was elected to the Missouri legislature in
1840. In 1849 he was back home, but again moved to
St. Louis in 1863 and was elected to the U.S. Senate in
1873, serving one term. He died in St. Louis in 1877.

Ste. Genevieve also was the home of the first U.S.
representative from Missouri, John Scott. He was
born in Virginia in 1785, educated at Princeton, and
then moved to Vincennes. With his move to Ste.
Genevieve in 1805 he became the town's first lawyer.
Despite his education, Scott rarely exhibited any sort
of refinement — a dirk and pistol were as much a part
of his raiment as his socks. He probably was one of the
court functionaries commented upon by Brackenridge
during his return visit to the old town in 1811. At that
time Brackenridge lamented the almost total loss of
gentility suffered by the town with the arrival of the

Americans. Scott is known to have worn his weapons in the courtroom, where he would continually bully both judge and jury into acquittals for some of the area's most villianous offenders.

Scott, as a member of the territorial legislature, was a guiding force in framing the first Missouri constitution, and in 1818 presented the petition for admission of Missouri as a state. He also is noted as the father of Missouri's public school system.

Scott was elected to Congress in 1821, where he served four terms. During his last term he found himself out of alignment with the forces opposing the reelection of John Quincy Adams to the presidency. His major opponent was the awesome Missouri senator, Thomas Hart Benton. Scott's political career, therefore, was concluded after that term of office. He returned to Ste. Genevieve to practice law until his death in 1861.

In the early part of the nineteenth century the population race between Ste. Genevieve and St. Louis was neck and neck. In 1752 there were twenty whites and three blacks in the town. In 1764, the year Laclede founded St. Louis, Ste. Genevieve had a population of 100 persons. Three years later, the flight of the Kaskaskians and other east bank residents from the British had raised this total to 350. By 1769 there were 600 in Ste. Genevieve, and in 1799 the figure was 949.

But St. Louis was catching up, thanks to aggressive recruiting activity by Auguste Chouteau. In 1799 St. Louis had only twenty-five persons fewer than Ste. Genevieve. In 1805 the population of the two towns was identical at 2,780. Ste. Genevieve's population remained there for the next century. St. Louis took off. The proximity of St. Louis to the mouth of the

Missouri made the difference — it rapidly became a base of departure for western exploration and commerce. By 1838, the last year of the beaver boom, St. Louis had a population in excess of 16,000, a figure that was to redouble many times as the great caravans outfitted for the West.

By 1960 Ste. Genevieve had grown to 3,992, up some 1,200 from the population of 1940. And more than one good citizen has expressed displeasure with such rapid expansion. In 1980 the figure was 4,450.

Ste. Genevieve would have been outstripped by St. Louis much earlier had it not been for Nouvelle Bourbon. A group of French nobles and nationals sympathetic to the cause of the Bourbons fled the old country during the revolution and settled in Gallipolis, Ohio. Recognizing that the young American democracy hardly would be as sympathetic toward a royalist cause as would the Spanish, they searched for a site west of the Mississippi, finally settling in an area next to the old *le grand champ* — atop the bluffs to the west, some two miles south of the new village. The year was 1793.

Leading the group was Don Pierre Carlos Delassus, father of Carlos Dehault Delassus, the man destined to become lieutenant governor of Upper Louisiana. There were only four or five actual members of the nobility in the settlement — but the rest had strong loyalist tendencies.

The New Bourbon territory encompassed an area from the Saline to the new settlement; from the big field west to Mine La Motte. In 1798 there were twenty houses on the town site, and a year later a census revealed there were 407 persons in the entire territory. The population reached a peak of 500 persons in 1799, then declined to nothing during the nineteenth century. There is no trace of the town today. But in 1794 it was sufficiently advanced to request a chapel (which it probably didn't get), and the following year a resident willed the community some ground for a hospital and endowed it with the proceeds from the sale of a number of fields nearby. The hospital didn't come through either.

For all the unusually high degree of civilization the French brought to the Mississippi Valley, they were unable to put formal education on a solid footing. They made several good tries, but in Ste. Genevieve it was an on-again, off-again proposition.

The first school in the old town probably was the one attended by young Henry Brackenridge. There is in the archives a will bearing a date of 1791, leaving a house and land for an orphanage and school. The location is unknown. The maker of the will was Madame Marguerite Peyroux de la Coudrenière. Brackenridge indicates that the school probably was in operation in 1792.

There was a period of seven years when the old town evidently was without either a school or the hope of getting one. But in December 1807, an organizational meeting was held marking the beginning of the Ste. Genevieve (Louisiana) Academy.

A fine ashlar stone building was erected on an eminence a few blocks from the heart of town and the first classes were held in the spring of 1810. Daniel Barry, the first instructor, proposed to teach English, French, Latin, Greek, mathematics, surveying, logic, metaphysics, geography, history, and natural and moral philosophy.

In the spring of 1812, Mann Butler, the noted

pioneer historian, came to Ste. Genevieve from Kentucky to assume the teaching chores. He lasted two years, after which the academy was closed.

A Swiss by the name of Joseph Hertick came to Ste. Genevieve in 1815 to found an academy in a rambling old house ten miles southwest of town. Called "The Asylum," the building provided an education for three future senators — Jones, Bogy, and Augustus Dodge, who married the schoolmaster's daughter. The institution ceased operation in 1830.

By 1819 the parish priest succeeded in gaining the services of three members of the Christian Brothers, headed by a Brother Antonin, to staff the Louisiana Academy. This was the first teaching facility of the Christian Brothers in America. The venture lasted but a few years.

Records indicate that some sort of school was in operation in the Price brick building, Third and Market streets, from 1824 through 1842.

Since the Louisiana Academy never had the depth of faculty to accommodate girls, the Sisters of Loretto opened an academy for girls in the two buildings built by Catherine Bolduc. She was the widowed daughter-in-law of Louis Bolduc. The structures had been erected for her son-in-law, Rene LeMeilleur, next door to the Bolduc House. A ten-foot-long passageway joined the two buildings — one of brick and the other frame. Our Lady of Mt. Carmel School was opened in 1837. The sisters sold the property eleven years later and purchased a tract at Fourth and Merchant, the site of the present convent of the Sisters of St. Joseph. They erected a convent and a classroom building. By 1858 the school had forty-two registered pupils.

The Louisiana Academy didn't achieve a solid

footing until Firmin Rozier took charge in 1849. He improved the building greatly and made an extensive brick addition in 1854. In 1861 he was listed as the principal and had four instructors working under him. The manpower drain caused by the Civil War resulted in the abandonment of the school in 1862.

While Ste. Genevieve was founded due to the fertility of its soil and its relationship to the Mississippi, it was sustained in later years by another factor — *El Camino Real,* the royal road. In past centuries it had been no more than an Indian trail, but by 1789 it was at least important enough to be given a name. People afoot or on horses considered it somewhat of a luxury, but the narrowness of the trace made travel by carriage or charette all but impossible.

El Camino Real began at New Madrid, passed through Cape Girardeau and Ste. Genevieve, and terminated somewhere near the riverfront in St. Louis. (The notion that Kingshighway Boulevard in the Central West End of St. Louis, was the terminal stretch of the old road seems erroneous— in 1789 this was a half-day's travel from the riverfront.) *El Camino Real* was declared a public

A stone marker on the west side of Third Street, between Merchant and Market, commemorates El Camino Real *— the Kingshighway — which led from New Madrid through Ste Genevieve to St. Louis.*

road by the Americans in 1807, and the Missouri
territorial legislature designated it as a postal route five
years later. The road generally followed the course of
U.S. Highway 61 through most of its 200-mile length.

The Mississippi River, great a boon as it was to
north-south travel, caused many a headache for those
who wanted merely to cross from one side to the other.
The Jesuit missionaries probably kept in excellent
physical condition negotiating the four or five miles of
water separating Kaskaskia from *le grand champ*.

John Price, the builder of the first brick building in
Missouri, was granted the right to operate a ferry between Ste. Genevieve and the east bank in 1798, but
there seems to be no evidence that he exercised it. An
earlier ferry definitely was in operation late in the
eighteenth century — by a man named Chailloux, *dit*
La Chance. A full-time ferry operation was undertaken in 1819 and appears to have operated sporadical-
ly until recent years. The ferries left Little Rock
Landing, at the foot of Maxwell's Hill some three
miles north of town, upon command.

A fine old steam railroad ferry was pulled out of
service at the same spot in the early 1960s after nearly a
century of service. (The railroad came to Ste.
Genevieve in June 1899.)

The big news on the river came in August 1817
when the steamer *General Pike,* Jacob Reed, captain,
passed by on her way to St. Louis. This was the
forerunner of the fabulous era that saw the St. Louis
harbor continuously choked with the frightening
goliaths. That the *Pike* passed Ste. Genevieve up for
St. Louis was indicative of the diminishing importance
of the old town as a port.

Not that the town lacked action. The steamers that
did tie up to take on wood did a brisk business from

The first train into Ste. Genevieve is shown the day it arrived, June 11, 1899.

townspeople eager to snap up the offerings from New Orleans.

The people of Ste. Genevieve had an opportunity to see the horror of steamboating too. One vessel, the *Franklin,* built in Pittsburgh in 1816, hit a snag and sank near Ste. Genevieve on her way from Louisville to St. Louis.

It was the demise of the *Dr. Franklin No. II* that shocked people. She was cruising about four miles north of town on August 22, 1852, when a flue collapsed. The result of the violent steam explosion is described by General Rozier;

Amongst the passengers was the famous novel writer Ned Buntline, who escaped unhurt. the sight on board of the steamer was a distressing and mournful one. The cabin of the boat was strewed with men and women, uttering the most fearful cries, and undergoing the most cruel sufferings. Strong men were blistered with steam, yet cold in death. Both engineers were blown into the river, and at the time of the explosion some jumped overboard and were lost. In one berth lay a wife and mother dead, with a child still clasped in her arms, whilst others were frightly mutilated. The citizens of Ste. Genevieve rendered all the aid and assistance to those unfortunate persons, and had the dead decently buried in the graveyard.

The death toll from the accident is variously estimated between twenty and thirty-two persons. The vessel survived the explosion, was rebuilt and ran the river until July 7, 1853, when she burned at the wharf in St. Louis. She was built at Wheeling, West Virginia, by John McLure in 1848. She was a small vessel, 173 feet long with a 26.5 beam, and drawing 4.3 feet of water.

The Mississippi had strange ways. Mark Twain, recalling his riverboat days in *Life on the Mississippi,* described an incident involving the capriciousness of the Mississippi channel. He was puzzled when his boat discharged a well-dressed family on a rocky point, with no evidence of civilization other than an old stone warehouse and two or three decaying houses. They set off afoot down a winding country road. Actually, they were bound for Ste. Genevieve, which had been shut in behind a new island, which has long since disappeared.

About the middle of the nineteenth century the Missouri legislature passed enabling laws for the formation of toll road companies. The entire state was in the grip of a plank road craze, and Ste. Genevieve was no exception. One was laid down from Iron Mountain to the old town during 1851-52. Plank roads were constructed by laying down parallel rails of round logs, then laying four-inch oak planks transversely over them. Maintaining the roadbed for forty miles was too expensive and the $200,000 cost never was recovered. Things were not going at all well for Ste. Genevieve. Soon the Iron Mountain Railroad had its direct line through to St. Louis — and the rich ore bypassed the old town entirely.

CHAPTER XII.

A Town Full of Excitement

The process of verifying old and relatively unimportant facts is laborious indeed, but proving something *didn't* happen is even more difficult.

For a century the rumor has circulated in Ste. Genevieve that the Marquis de Lafayette stopped overnight in town and slept on the old spool bed in the house of Commandant J. B. Vallé.

In 1825 General Lafayette accepted an invitation from the United States to visit the nation he had helped so much during the American Revolution.

It was in mid-April of that year that he left New Orleans, bound for an unscheduled trip to St. Louis. It is known that on Wednesday, April 27, the steamer *Natchez*, with Lafayette aboard, stopped "for a few hours" in Cape Girardeau. It is verified that the boat tied up for the evening at 5 o'clock April 28 in Cardondelet. The general arrived at the foot of Market Street in St. Louis at 9 A.M. April 29. He spent the day going from one reception to another, but he boarded the *Natchez* to spend the night, as had been his custom throughout the journey. It is certain that he took lunch in Kaskaskia on April 30, on his way back downstream.

Had Captain Davis tied up the *Natchez* at Cape Girardeau at 7 A.M. on the twenty-seventh, and had the "few hours" been, say, four, then it is possible that she could have made Ste. Genevieve by 9 P.M. She could have left at 8 A.M. the following day and made Carondelet by 5 P.M.

There has been no verification of the rumor that the general was accompanied throughout his voyage by a mysterious twenty-four-year-old woman, a circumstance which might have accounted for his insistence in remanding aboard the *Natchez* every night.

Ste. Genevieve did have one internationally distinguished visitor — Otho, King of Greece, a world class freeloader.

Otho had been king of the Hellenes only three years when, at the age of twenty, he decided to visit America. In 1835 he arrived at the doorstep of John Jacob Astor, then a partner in the American Fur Company, in New York. The busy Astor used his great persuasive powers to encourage the young playboy to visit the hinterlands, specifically St. Louis, and his partner, Pierre Chouteau.

No mean talker himself, Chouteau persuaded his highness that for real fun he should see Ste. Genevieve, and stay with *his* friend, Jean Baptiste Vallé, the aging commandant.

And so the strapping, six-foot buffoon spent the next three months taxing the patience and good manners of Vallé, Gen. Jean Baptiste Bossier, and others of the gentle French.

Otho was the last of the big spenders. He played cards for high stakes and, being rather thick, he lost considerably more often than he won. He was in no danger of losing his stake, however, because his adversaries were far to polite to take money from royalty.

He was forever badgering General Bossier to shoot pigeons with him at $5 a bird, and Bossier was forever thinking up excuses to avoid the shoot. There really wasn't any money involved — Otho couldn't hit a bird if he held it in his left hand and shot at it with his right.

Even an energetic young monarch like Otho could get tired, and after three months he headed back to Greece, again by way of Chouteau, who convinced him that the real action was back in New York. Astor told him to keep right on going, and sure enough, Otho found some excitement right at home in Greece. He was deposed in 1862.

Mob violence never visited Ste. Genevieve. There was violence, however, in the form of two notable duels.

The first occurred on October 1, 1811, on Moreau's Island, opposite Ste. Genevieve. Thomas T. Crittenden, a young lawyer from Kentucky, was successful in his defense of a man accused of slander by Ezekiel Fenwick. Dr. Walter Fenwick, brother of the accuser, challenged the attorney and fell mortally wounded.

Another duel took place on the steps of the territorial courthouse in August 1816. Auguste De Mun, a candidate for the territorial legislature, had made certain comments in the community about the alleged counterfeiting activities of his opponent, William McCarthur, a brother-in-law of Dr. Linn. McCarthur sent his challenge, which De Mun refused. When McCarthur insulted De Mun publicly they met at the courthouse. While court was in session McCarthur went down the steps and De Mun went up. At a signal they whirled and fired. De Mun lost. He is buried in the old cemetery in Ste. Genevieve, sans tombstone.

A photo taken during the flood of 1881 shows the Mississippi swirling about an old Kaskaskia house.

Thereafter, the periods of excitement were few. There was the great flood of 1844 — even worse than the one in *L'anée de grandes eaux,* 1785. Then the waters completely filled the lowlands, from Missouri cliffs to the valley wall in Illinois. Some two-and-one-half feet higher than the waters of 1785, the river at some places was nine miles wide. Kaskaskia was more than eight feet under water. Francis Rozier supposedly dived off a retaining wall at Main and Merchant into several feet of water. Farmers went to bed in one state and woke up in another.

Excitement was again stirred up during the great bank robbery of 1873. On May 26 four bad guys knocked off the Rozier bank — their shotguns and navy revolvers minimizing any resistance.

The *Ste. Genevieve Fair Play* ganged their headlines as follows:

DARING ROBBERY !!!!
A FOUR THOUSAND DOLLAR HAUL !!!!
Four Men Walked Into the Merchants Bank of Ste.
Genevieve in Open Day Light and Robbed the Safe of
its Contents and Escaped !!!!
The Cashier Was Forced at the Muzzle of Two Pistols
to Open the Safe.
GREAT EXCITEMENT !!!!
CITIZENS TURN OUT EN MASSE IN PURSUIT
OF THE THIEVES !!!!
The report carried in the St. Louis *Missouri
Republican* described the event in detail:

> If there is any operation in which the
> audaciousness of pure devilry ever be
> displayed, it is in the exercise of high art in
> robbing a bank in broad daylight. Occasional-
> ly within late years whole communities have
> thrilled with the daring deeds of men whose
> intent to plunder has been consummated
> under circumstances requiring forethought,
> skill, nerve, and dispatch. Midnight robbery
> has all the elements of wicked romance, but it
> does not begin to excite those emotions of sur-
> prise that startle business circles when crime is
> perpetrated in the immediate presence of
> witnesses in the bright light of day. The
> chronicles of the times are prolific with
> accounts of what desperate men dare to do:
> but perhaps there has been no greater exhibi-
> tion of boldness than that which was displayed
> yesterday in the quiet town of Ste. Genevieve,
> Mo., on the Mississippi River.

> The bank, situated upon the corner of Mer-
> chant Street and Main, stands a two-story

brick house used as a banking house by the Ste. Genevieve Savings Association. Gen. Firmin A. Rozier is President and O. D. Harris cashier.

The hour for commencing business is 10 o'clock in the morning. As usual Mr. Harris went to the bank yesterday, and having opened the front door, laid the safe keys on his desk nearby. He then walked to the front door of the building, where he engaged in conversation with General Rozier's son, who had come to the bank. Soon a gentleman named Herzog approached. While the three men were talking two men on foot, strangers to them, were observed on the street passing by. Mr. Herzog soon left, but he had not gone fifty yards distant when the strangers retraced their steps.

How the Robbers Operated.

Seeing that they intended to enter the bank, Mr. Harris preceded them, the whole party followed by young Rozier. When half way in the room the cashier happened to turn his head and was startled at [the] sight of two pistols pointed to his temples, and was most thoroughly aroused to the delicacy of the situation as he felt the cold muzzles quickly pressed to them. The force used by the robbers was so great that for hours afterwards one of his temples showed the mark of the pistol barrel. Before he could remonstrate he was saluted with a stirring command. "Open the safe or I'll blow your d . . . d brains out." Mr. Harris hesitated about opening the safe, which being observed, caused the robbers to level their pistols at Rozier, threatening to shoot him if he should run. But Rozier broke away and was confronted by two other men on horseback, who were concealed from observation.

Pistol Practice

These fellows fired three shots, putting a ball through Rozier's coat, close to the shoulder. A Negro happened to witness the scene, but dared to do nothing more than fold his arms and stand still under cover of a pistol held by one of the horsemen, who threatened to kill him if he moved a hairsbreadth.

Inside of the Treasure Box.

While this attempted tragedy was being played on the street, the pinioned cashier was involuntarily performing his quiet part in the bank by receiving a blow from the butt of a pistol. The two robbers drew him to the safe, which he opened. Then they made a grab for the first valuables, securing about three thousand dollars in currency. They also grasped a cash box which they supposed held bonds and other papers of value. It happened, however, to contain the papers of ex-sheriff R. G. Madison, who is now a state representative. The box also contained one hundred dollars in gold. They then overhauled other papers belonging to the bank, but not representing money. Finding that time was precious, the two desperadoes jerked Mr. Harris' watch from his vest-pocket and then grasped him by the coat collar, still pointing their pistols at his head, and marched him out of the bank building toward the standing place of the two waiting thieves outside about a square off.

Street Shooting

At this place one of the horses had been tied to a tree, but had gotten loose. Just then a German citizen came along, when the thieves shouted to him "Hitch that horse, G . d d . . . n you. If you don't I'll shoot you." The German obeyed orders.

The robbers speedily released Mr. Harris, mounted their horses, and the four commenced firing in all direction to intimidate pursuers. Above the reports of the shots was heard a wild "Hurrah for Sam Hildebrand, catch the horse thieves if you can," and then the rapid hoofbeats of the retreating horses showed that the job was finished.

The Robbers took the Perryville road, and when a short distance out opened Mr. Madison's box and extricated the gold. They met a German farmer and asked him if he had any money. He replied "No." "Oh well," said one of the men, "I guess you're poor. Go down the road and you will find a box with papers in it. Take it to the bank and they will give you a hundred dollars." The German returned the box to the bank and reported the circumstances, but failed to collect the hundred dollars.

The Pursuit

The above transactions were conducted with all the celerity demanded by the exigencies, and in a shorter time than required for description. Young Rozier sounded the alarm as soon as possible, but the only men on the streets were halted by the pistols of the robbers, and did not dare to move hands or feet in attempting capture. By the time he did secure assistance the scamps had gone.

While the robbery was going on a gentleman, who lived in a house opposite to the bank, saw it, and had his revolver elevated to shoot across the street into the bank, but his wife begged him to desist, fearing the robbers in revenge would shoot Mr. Harris. Thus they escaped their just desserts, and went out of town with all the bravado of impudent horsethieves and burglars.

That the whole affair was well planned there can be no doubt. Two of the robbers slept the night before at a farm house two miles out. They knew that Gen. Rozier, the president, whose room is on the same floor with the bank floor, was absent. They also supposed, and rightly, that in that town of 1,500 inhabitants only a few persons would be in the streets at the hour for bank opening. They also supposed that the safe would be unlocked immediately after the opening of the bank, thus facilitating their stealing.

As might be expected, the people of Ste. Genevieve were greatly excited by the robbery. As soon as possible a bank of mounted men organized, and armed with shotguns went in pursuit of the robbers. Chief McDonough was last night informed of this robbery, and will set his police machinery in motion to secure information.

The robbery, though one of the boldest on record, did not pan out very handsomely, as the booty amounted to only $3,600. This was all the bank lost, no bonds having been taken.

Later newspapers fail to mention anything of the robbery or the robbers — evidently the thieves never were apprehended.

There evidently is no truth to the rumor that the bandits were headed by Jesse James, or that they stopped in the barn behind the house of Commandant Vallé to divvy up the loot. Jesse was a vain robber and had a way of autographing his art so there would be little doubt about who did the dirt.

CHAPTER XIII.

Ste. Genevieve Rediscovered

As has been said, the growth of Ste. Genevieve was arrested by a number of factors, most of them prompted by the better geography of St. Louis. There can't be much truth to the supposition that the supposed indolence of the French caused the decline. In the early days the town prospered mightily under the French, indolent or not. The old town, like any number of others in the Middle Valley, was inundated with industrious Germans in the immigration wave of 1825-45. By the middle of the nineteenth century there were far more Germans there than French, and English had become the domestic tongue of both national groups.

Gradually agriculture grew in importance. *Le grand champ* continued its fabulous production, as indeed it does today. The tough, dedicated Germans cleared the land to the west and agriculture became big business.

It became big business everywhere else too, and as modern technology started catching up with its potential, the marginal farm disappeared, and so did the marginal farmer.

But fortune smiled upon Ste. Genevieve, as it had done so many times before. Industry arrived, and with it the sort of stability that appears to be permanent.

The vast deposits of limestone west of town were purchased by Mississippi Lime Company early in the twentieth century, and soon the firm had built up the old quarry to the point where it became one of the world's largest producers of lime. Chemical quicklime, chemical hydrate, precipitated calcium carbonate, and various sizes of limestone are produced there.

The Mississippi Lime Company has showered the people of Ste. Genevieve with civic benevolence. More than one-fourth of the town's wage earners work there, and the firm has consistently recognized its obligation to them. The company saved the Bolduc House when it seemed that no one else cared. They saved and restored the Linden House across the street, and as the second floor balconies sagged and fell, signifying the imminent end of the Bolduc-LeMeilleur House (the old Loretto convent), Mississippi Lime saved that one too.

Other industries also have contributed to the prosperity. General Pass Book Company, one of the world's largest producers of checkbook covers and passbooks for banks and savings institutions, has been succeeded by Sylvanus Products. Their plant is highly sophisticated and embodies more printing techniques under one roof than any in St. Louis.

Bilt-Best Corporation came to town with a new plant, bringing with it orders for preglazed window sash for residential construction, and that company is growing rapidly. Selmor Manufacturing Company, diversifying its St. Louis production facilities, located a factory in the west end of town to produce shirts and various other clothing items. Kisco Boiler produces steel tanks and other vessels for industry. The industrial growth is continuing.

There has been no lack of appreciation of this heritage on the part of the people of Ste. Genevieve. July 21, 1885, was the day selected for the celebration of the 100th anniversary of the move to the new town, and the 150th anniversary of what the people then believed to be the year of the town's founding.

They had no trouble waking people up that Tuesday morning. The St. Louis Cavalry and Artillery, a military company, bought its cannon down for the occasion and fired the national salute of twenty-one rounds at 6:30 A.M. The *Will S. Hays* carried a load of visitors from St. Louis, the *Bellefontaine* came over from Chester, and the *Nick Swaer* arrived from Kaskaskia. The Ste. Genevieve Cornet Band led the long procession to Maxwell's Hill, just above Little Rock Landing, and included in the line were the mayor, city officers, clergymen, county officers, the visitors, the townspeople, and an elaborate float constructed by the ladies of the town.

At Maxwell's Hill the flags of France, Spain, and the United States were unfurled and the artillery boomed. General Rozier, Alex. J. P. Garesche, Col. F. T. Lederberger, Maj. William Cozzens, and Lyndon A. Smith, secretary to Mayor David R. Francis of St. Louis, also boomed.

Merciful Providence intervened at four o'clock, when the heavens opened up, drenching the fiery orators with such a cloudburst that more than a few of the people wondered if *L'anné des grandes eaux* weren't about to repeat itself. It was a day to remember.

Those who are supposed to know about these things

say that there never was any celebration anywhere, before or since, to rival the bicentennial celebration in Ste. Genevieve in 1935.

Considering the size of the town, the magnitude of the effort is a little startling to this day. Meetings were started in January 1933 to plan the pageant. The Missouri legislature felt justified in appropriating $10,000, since this was the oldest town in the state. This sum was supplemented by pledges from over 100 of the townspeople.

Historic research was started more than two years in advance of the celebration. Orchestral and choral rehearsals were begun more than a year in advance. Twenty-four local dance instructors assisted a professional choreographer in teaching several hundred children the routines called for in the script. Volunteers sewed three hundred juvenile costumes, and as many adult costumes were rented. Men, women, and children from all over the county were assigned parts. The cast numbered 1,200.

The Vallé Spring, just southwest of town, was the site of the pageant. The little stream was dammed to form a miniature Mississippi, and the natural amphitheater was large enough to hold the 15,000 people who jammed in to see the spectacle. A three-level stage was built, and an elaborate lighting complex was installed. A "Goddess of Liberty" was erected to oversee the affair, and she was upstaged by a huge lighted cross.

Back in town, the people were encouraged to bedeck their homes and businesses with the colors of the three nations that had ruled over this land. Medallions were sold all over the United States as souvenirs. An area encompassing the entire state and southern Illinois was deluged with bumper strips, posters, literature, and press releases. The chamber of commerce brought one state convention after another to town in 1935, preparing the merchants for the crushing crowds that were to come in late August. Workmen rushed the little stone museum to completion.

The celebration opened on August 19, 1935, with a Pontifical High Mass celebrated by the auxiliary bishop of St. Louis. The mayor and other civic officials delivered appropriate remarks that afternoon, and later in the day the new Ste. Genevieve museum was dedicated.

That night the first five episodes of the pageant took place. They were narrated over a public address system by a professional reader — there was no dialogue. Thus ended Ste. Genevieve Day.

On the second day, St. Louis Day, Bernard F. Dickmann, mayor of St. Louis, was the guest of honor, and five more episodes were enacted that night. August 21, 1935, was Missouri Day. Governor and Mrs. Guy Brasfield Park were overshadowed by the presence of the U. S. Sixth Infantry and Regimental Band, sixteen state bands and bugle corps, and a score of historical floats.

National Day was the name given to the finale, when the French consul to the U.S. addressed the throngs. That night, President Franklin D. Roosevelt talked to the assemblage via amplified telephone: ''We hail the stalwart qualities of frontier days, and the Christian courage of our pioneers . . . it is with full appreciation of your past that, on this occasion of your Bicentennial celebration, I extend to you my hearty wishes for a happy and prosperous future.''

The Mississippi is still a mixed blessing. *Le grand*

champ will be flooded again and again, and the levees on the upper Missouri and the Mississippi will direct the floods back to unprotected Ste. Genevieve. The ferry still operates from Little Rock Landing, and will continue to do so until a hoped-for bridge across the broad Mississippi is built.

But Ste. Genevieve is like a drowsy giant. It is only a matter of a few years before the American people, restless for "new" old things to see, will learn of Ste. Genevieve. Gone will be the sleepy Sundays when a dozen St. Louisans drove to the old town to buy a sundae and gawk at the wonderful old homes. Interstate 55 is bringing perhaps hundreds of thousands of people a year from St. Louis. Traffic will jam from time to time and the city fathers gradually will get things organized.

Five will get you ten that the charisma will remain, despite the throngs, the balloons, the souvenirs. People still will be able to leave the new downtown hotel at midnight, walk past the darkened homes, stare up at the brillant firmament and wonder what those stars have seen. The magic is there. It will never leave.

Epilogue

The changes which have swept over Ste. Genevieve in the two decades since this book was first published — or even in the ten years since the appearance of the third edition — are remarkable.

The year 1973 has displaced 1785 as *l'anne des grandes eaux*. The great river boiled over its banks on April 28 to 43.31 feet over flood stage. Volunteers worked around the clock for several days to protect the old town, and only because of this there was very little damage to the historic houses. One of the lowest, the Amoureux, became virtually an island, but it did remain dry if not high.

The inundation was frightening. Aircraft were over Kaskaskia Island when the first levee gave way. The brown ribbon of water sped across the island at startling speed, crashed against the inside of the opposite levee, and then splayed out across the entire island. Soon almost everything was submerged.

The devastation in Ste. Genevieve prompted an outcry for a major flood protection program. This was endorsed by the Corps of Engineers, purely on the grounds of historic preservation. That was a first for the Corps. A $33.6-million program was proposed in 1985, but so far there has been no action.

The St. Louis office of the Corps of Engineers — specifically F. Terry Norris — has been active in the archaeology of the old town. It had heretofore been believed that the flooding Mississippi had long ago washed away all evidence of the old town. Norris, unwilling to accept this, has proved the opposite is true. The river in fact protected the evidence by covering it with thick layers of silt.

Norris and his colleagues revealed that many of the early suppositions about the building patterns were true. However, the lots weren't contiguous. Two or three habitations were built alongside each other along the riverbank, then there was open space, then one or two more houses — for more than a mile along the water's edge. There was no sign of the mysterious well, nor of Papa Vallé's grave. But funding was available for only a superficial study. The definitive dig has yet to take place.

The site is privately owned and the landowner has pledged to prosecute unauthorized visitors.

Perhaps the most significant event during the last decade was the celebration of the town's 250th anniversary in 1985. Despite Carl Ekberg's research which revealed that the founding date was about 1750, Ste. Genevieve decided to celebrate anyway. "Look at it this way," one resident said, "it is the golden anniversary of the bicentennial celebration."

Led by the indefatigable Bernard K. Schram, the year-long observance resulted in a massive amount of publicity — gaining even international attention — for Ste. Genevieve. Of greater importance, it brought many Missourians an awareness of the international importance of the leading historical town in their state. Ste. Genevieve was even featured in the official 1985-86 Missouri road map.

During the 250th year several scholarly convocations met to discuss the old town. The grant money raised was significant, as scholars assembled known facts and uncovered new ones about the town. Many reports have yet to be filed. Osmond Overby, the noted architectural historian from the university of Missouri at Columbia, led a building study program, including some borings in the logs of most of the old houses. The tree-ring dating indicated that most of the structures were not as old as the traditional dates, but that they were very old indeed.

The culminating event of the celebration was the release of Carl J. Ekberg's book, *Colonial Ste. Genevieve: An Adventure on the Mississippi Frontier.* Many residents are unconvinced of the accuracy of his founding date, despite his thorough demolition of the stories that have been handed down. Some residents, and all major scholars in Missouri and of French Colonial history in the world, have accepted his study as fact. The book has won several major prizes in American history and gained excellent reviews in scholarly periodicals.

Much of the 1966 AEA report which started this book was viewed as pie-in-the-sky. One facet, especially, was viewed with jaundiced eyes — the paving of historic streets with cobblestone and the burial of utility lines. Persistent citizens have secured grant funds to resurface many of the old streets, provide specially designed "antique" street lights, install exposed aggregate sidewalks, plant trees, and install street furniture throughout the historic area. All this has resulted in a new "old" look for the town. At the end of a transformed Market Street is the new Great River Road Interpretive Center—designed by architect Jack Luer and constructed in the tradition of the pioneer French. The Misselhorn Gallery is a permanent exhibit of remarkable sketches of Ste. Genevieve by the venerable Roscoe Misselhorn, some made a generation ago. The main gallery has changing exhibits pertaining to the pioneer French. A call to (314) 883-7097 will produce an interesting packet of information on Ste. Genevieve.

Thus, the town which never seems to change is in fact changing all the time. Unlike other places, Ste. Genevieve changes in two directions—forward in civic services and accommodations for visitors; backward in the recreation of the interpretation of the past.

And through it all the great eighteenth-century buildings still stand, impassive reminders of what has been, and of the importance of saving them so that future generations will know where we have been.

The Great River Road Interpretive Center serves as a focus for visitors to Ste. Genevieve.

Appendix 1

There are more than thirty major tourist attractions in or near Ste. Genevieve, and it is the purpose of this appendix to enrich the experience of viewing each of them.

They are listed in the order which should be of maximum interest and convenience to the average visitor, and that is not necessarily the order of importance to architects, historians, townspeople, or the author.

Since the community is small, most of these sites may be reached on foot. Automobiles are necessary in visiting only nine of them.

There are perhaps a dozen important homes which have not been cited. Placed in any major midwestern city, any one of them would attract a great deal of attention. They are not listed here because their importance pales when they are pitted against the great houses which are listed. An example might be that of the famous DeMenil house in south St. Louis. If the DeMenil, which is a fine house indeed, were in Ste. Genevieve it would not make the list. Nor would it be a candidate for restoration. There are too many older homes in Ste. Genevieve that would precede it in importance.

A matter of some concern is the dating of the old houses. With only one or two exceptions, all buildings have been given differing completion dates by the various reference works. Usually the dates were off only a year or two, but on occasion a discrepancy of five to ten years was noted. An almost universal lack of legal documentation of erection dates forced the acceptance of the consensus of more learned authorities.

Generally, the creole houses may be classified structurally by their French terms: *maison de poteaux en terre* (house with posts into the earth), *maison de poteaux sur solle* (house with posts on a sill), and *maison de pierre* (house of stone). The Anglo-American houses generally were framed with lap siding.

Strangely enough, the *poteaux en terre* technique is known neither in France nor in Canada. Most likely it was brought up from the Gulf Coast — the dwellings of the Indians who had used the method in the area had been gone for hundreds of years.

Glass for the windows of the older homes had to be imported from Europe. The few bricks that were used probably came from New Orleans kilns. The stone, of course, came from the bluffs.

There are two most interesting homes that should be listed here but cannot be — they were destroyed in recent years. One is the home of Francis Rozier, on the northeast corner of Merchant and Main. The mansion was torn down about 1958. It is said that young Rozier dived off a retaining wall (which still remains) into the waters of the flood in 1844.

The Misplait house, alleged to have been moved

Courtesy Ida M. Schaaf

This is the last known photo of the old Misplait house, torn down in the 1940s. Said to have been located on le grand champ, *the Misplait allegedly was moved to a tract just north of the Amoureux house, on the west side of St. Marys Road, just after the flood of 1785.*

from *le grand champ,* was located along old St. Marys Road, just north of the Amoureux house. It was demolished in the late 1940s.

To become oriented, it is best to use Main Street as a baseline. It runs north and south across South Gabouri Creek and becomes St. Marys Road. Located along this street, from north to south, are the Inn St. Gemme Beauvais on the east side, the Ste. Genevieve Hotel on the west side, the Beauvais on the east, the J. B. Vallé, Bolduc-LeMeilleur, and Bolduc on the west, and the Linden house on the east side.

(See map, inside back cover.)

Just north of the low water bridge across the Gabouri, on the east side, is the Ratte-Hoffman house and the Moses Austin cabin. Across the creek, on the west, are the Janis-Ziegler house (Green Tree Tavern), Misplait site, Amoureux house, and the Bequette-Ribault house. *Le grand champ* is on the east.

The principal streets from the Gabouri north, intersecting Main Street, are South Gabouri, Market, Merchant, Jefferson, and Washington. Paralleling Main Street are Second, Third, Fourth, and Fifth streets. It would take three full days to see all there is to see in this area alone, and it all can be reached afoot.

Bolduc House
West side of Main, between Market and
South Gabouri streets

Louis Bolduc (1734-1815), a lead miner, merchant, and planter, was born in Canada. He became a wealthy Ste. Genevieve landowner and slave holder, and his descendants lived in this house until the 1940s.

This is the first known example of an authentic and essentially complete French creole house in the

The Bolduc house.

Mississippi Valley being restored to its original form.

The structure, in dilapidated condition, was acquired in 1949 by the National Society of Colonial Dames of America as a gift to the Missouri Society. It

West gallery of the Bolduc house

was restored in 1956-57, under the direction of the noted Ernest Allen Connally.

For a number of years architectural historians supposed that the Bolduc was really two cabins — this was based upon the observation that the ceiling construction and height in the two principal rooms was different. Connally, however, noted that the stone foundations are a continuous and uniform structure, as are the exterior walls and the roof framing, establishing that the house was one construction.

Connally said that the ceiling construction differed because of a need to use the attic for storage of heavy goods, possibly lead. He stated "At some time, quite early, it was used to store corn. We found highly dessicated, blackened, shriveled

The restored kitchen-bakehouse at the rear of the Bolduc house.

corncobs in some cracks. Such storage would have been fairly easy, since there was originally no ceiling in the *galerie.*''

Connally can only guess at the date of construction.

The rear of the Bolduc house from the orchard shows old boxwoods in a formal garden and a brick kitchen under the gallery at left.

The Ste. Genevieve archives hold a contract for a house dated 1769 that approaches the size of the Bolduc, but still is somewhat smaller, with a narrow, floorless *galerie.* Certainly it was built in the old town. Another contract, between Louis Boisleduc and Louis Boulet, dated 1770, is for a building about (but not exactly) half the size of the Bolduc — twenty-six feet by twenty-one feet six inches, with a narrow gallery all around.

Connally doubts that either house is a part of the existing Bolduc, but he admits to the possibility that some of the heavy timbers from houses on the old site might have been used. ''It was a lot of work to hew out heavy timbers, and roof trusses could be disassembled and moved.''

He doubts the supposition that the old house

Simple, rugged furniture, often homemade, graced the early French homes in Ste. Genevieve. This is the Bolduc dining room.

was moved up from *le grand champ* after the flood. "I think it quite likely that it could have been built initially on the present site as late as 1785-90. Such a late date would in no way detract from the importance of the house, which remains one of the largest, oldest, and most instructive examples of French colonial architecture in the upper Mississippi Valley." Tree ring studies in 1986 indicate that the principal structural members were about that age.

It is not certain that Bolduc built the house, but he was living there at the time of his death. In 1815 the property extended northward to Market Street. The lot transfer records show that some of the Bolduc ancillary structures stood on the lot where the Bolduc-LeMeilleur house is now. Connally found the stone foundations of a small square on the contemporary property line and assumes they were the remains of the original kitchen building. Since most of the old foundations were on the Bolduc-LeMeilleur lot in 1815, the Bolduc house would have been without a kitchen when the Bolduc-LeMeilleur was erected, about 1820. Connally presumes, therefore, that the northwest corner of the *galerie* was enclosed at that time to make a kitchen. It is presumed also, from the structural

This cabinet, now in the Bolduc house, is said to have survived the flood of 1785. There are water stains on the lower part of the doors.

evidence, that the *galerie* ceiling was added then, too.

The Bolduc consists essentially of two large rooms separated by a central hall — all surrounded by the *galerie*. The outside dimensions of the total house are forty-eight feet by eighty-two feet. It is covered by a steeply pitched hip roof, which changes to a more flat slope over the *galeries*. The walls are of heavy oak timbers set upright on a stone foundation. Six-inch interstices between the posts are filled with a nogging of clay and chopped straw *(bouzillage)*. The walls are whitewashed.

The roof is supported by heavy oak trusses of the same type used in Normandy in the middle ages.

Smaller versions of the buildings which might have been on the lot have been added to the rear of the Bolduc. A formal garden and orchard are miniatures of the original. Sprigs from the boxwoods and food stuffs prepared from the produce of the land are sold at the site by the Colonial Dames, operators of the house. Funding of the restoration was aided by the late Constance A. and Harry B. Mathews, Jr.

The furnishings in the house are authentic antiques — many of them dating back to the eighteenth century. Included is a cupboard (or armoire) showing a stain about two feet above the floor, allegedly caused by the flood of 1785. Inside the door is the date, 1735. The authenticity of both marks is to be doubted. The flood of 1785 didn't stop two feet above the floor (although the house in which the piece rested may have been on higher ground), and the 1735 date could have been added by a budding public relations man at any time.

Still, the house, its furnishings and grounds constitute a towering example of French colonial living and architecture in the late eighteenth century. It is unquestionably the best known historic house in the Middle Valley, and one which has earned the respect of architectural historians everywhere.

The Bolduc is open to the public from April 1 to November 1, 10 A.M. to 4 P.M. daily. A small admission fee is charged.

St. Gemme-Amoureux House
St. Marys Road ⅓ mile south of South Gabouri Creek

Occupied after 1800 by Mathurin Michel Amoureux, a French nobleman and a correspondent of Albert Gallatin and Thomas Jefferson, this house was long believed to have been built by Jean Baptiste St. Gemme Beauvais about 1770, then moved from *le grand champ* soon after the flood of 1785. This point was disputed by Charles E. Peterson, and the 1986 tree ring studies indicate the timbers were harvested in 1792.

Unlike the Bolduc, the Amoureux is a working house It has a tin roof — cedar shakes or especially the authentic thatch would cause severe fire risk problems. Since the old house is used as a museum and an antique shop, the owners felt justified in the installation of air conditioning. Yet, the Amoureux is a splendid example of a French creole house — care has been taken to assure that the installation of unauthentic improvements was done in a manner which would not detract excessively from the historical presentation. One notable exception is the use of brick on the portions of the chimneys projecting above the roof — a situation the owners intend to correct.

The house is *poteaux en terre* construction — handhewn cedar logs are clearly visible beneath the

The Amoureux house

These great oak beams are reinforced by rubble stone buttresses in the Amoureux foundation.

front *galerie* and in the earthen cellar. The roof has a typical steep Canadian pitch (seventy-two degrees) at the peak, flattening out to fifty-two degrees over the *galeries*.

The Amoureux has been examined by experts in the field of historic preservation who are unanimous in their opin-

This old walnut fireplace in the Amoureux house was beneath several layers of paint and varnish.

Ancient strap hinges— one fishtail, the other rattail—are believed to be the original hardware for the Amoureux cellar door.

ion that it was built originally without *galeries* and that the roof was thatched. There still are nail holes in the members of the ponderous Norman truss which go down to the plate. Remnants of thatching strips were found in 1966.

The roof framing has been cut off on the west end of the house where the wall is constructed in the American manner. Thus it may be concluded that the house originally extended farther to the west (Connally thinks about twelve feet). It is believed that a remodeling took place not long after the initial construction. It involved the addition of the *galeries* and possibly the clapboard siding.

It was the custom of the French builders to eliminate as many of the sharp edges as possible. Even though it required hours of handwork, the edges of the walnut beams on the ceiling are beaded throughout.

Layers of plaster were chipped away from the entrance hall by the owner to expose what is believed to be the original pumpkin pine paneling. A huge walnut mantle in the living room was brought out from beneath several layers of paint and varnish.

To the rear of the house, over the site of the original west wall, the owner has added a "country store" in the Norman tradition, outfitting it with antique store fixtures from the area.

From the one *galerie* which remains, visitors may gain a commanding view of *le grand champ,* just across the St. Marys Road.

The name is spelled "Amoureaux" in Ste. Genevieve, but it appears as "Amoureux" in the family papers in the Ste. Genevieve archives.

The house is open during most warm weather days, usually for tours. A small admission fee is charged throughout the year, with tours conducted by the owner, Mrs. Frankye Donze. (This was the first of six Ste. Genevieve properties restored by Frankye and the late Norbert B. Donze. None was funded by grants.)

Jean Baptiste Vallé House

Northwest corner, Main and Market streets

The late Guy Study, a noted St. Louis traditional

architect, called the J. B. Vallé "the most important house in town." From an architect's standpoint this could hardly be true, but for the historian is most assuredly is. This was the social hub of the new town. The big decisions were made here, for J. B. Vallé

The Jean Baptiste Vallé house

(1760-1849) was the last of the commandants — for only four days under the Spanish and later under the Americans. There is much doubt that the basement of this house was constructed to serve as a fortress, as was believed earlier.

A substantial number of sources state the superstructure of the house was moved up from *le grand champ* in 1782, some three years before the flood. This seems improbable too, even though the river was causing considerable distress at the time. The 1986 tree ring study indicates that the house was built new just where it is, in 1794.

Possibly it was built by François Vallé II — there are some who say it was used as a Spanish state house until 1804. If that is true, it had to have been occupied by François II, because he was the commandant until his death in 1804. Yet, it is known that François Vallé built and occupied the house bearing his name on the

Gabouri immediately after the flood.

It also is possible that J. B. built the place and it became the statehouse after the death of his brother.

The J.B. Vallé house was never unoccupied. Consequently, as the technology of living improved, so did the house. Drastic changes were effected before its purchase by Leon Vion in the 1860s and they were be-

The rear-quarter view of the J.B. Vallé house shows the maid's quarters to the left of the gallery in the foreground.

One corner of the J. B. Vallé basement is occupied by a room with massive stone walls, once believed to be the foundation for an old fort.

ing made even in the 1960s. Through it all, the owners seem to have been deeply conscious of the history of the great house, and have been careful to make only those alternations considered fundamental to modern living. The house still retains its inherent grace.

The walls of the basement "fort" are of rubblestone, three to four feet thick. Wedges have been driven to keep the forty-six-foot oak beams from sagging. The room has corners bulging with three-quarter-round masonry buttresses, complete with loopholes. The area now is used for storage.

Across the hall from the "fort" is a room rumored to have served as a dungeon — the flat bars still are at the window. The owners, however, feel that the room was always for food storage; the barred window was for the admission of fresh air and security against human and animal thieves. It makes an excellent storage room for canned goods. The adjacent wine room still serves its original purpose, and some of the empty bottles found there dated back 100 years. Beside one of the interior partitions there still rests an old steamer truck bearing the name "L. Vion."

Courtesy Vera Okenfuss

The main floor houses a parlor on the right and a library on the left, separated by a deep center hall leading to the rear rooms. Behind the library is a bedroom, housing the "Lafayette" spool bed. To the right is the dining room, and off that a large kitchen, which was added in later years. A small sunporch now is located along the north gallery, overlooking a splendid garden. Along the west gallery are the maid's bedroom, now used as the owner's

Poteaux sur solle *construction is revealed beneath the plaster of the J. B. Vallé house. The great oak posts of such houses were slanted in the corners to provide extra rigidity through triangulation.*

study. The first floor ceilings are supported by oak beams forty-six feet long.

The second floor, believed to have been used as a granary, now is punctuated with dormers. It once was dominated by a whopping old Norman truss, removed when the second level was converted to living quarters.

Leon Vion came from France in the 1840s and bought the J. B. Vallé house in 1867. Extensive modifications were made to the roof, including the installation of the dormers and the bricking of the six chimneys. Handsome oak shelving was added to the library, and the interior partitioning was rearranged to form the added rooms. Although the kitchen probably had been moved up under the gallery by that time, Vion modernized it and added more space in other areas beneath the galleries. He embellished the interior with handsome brass cornices and valances.

There was no changing the walls. The rear oak posts exert their elephantine weight against the unyielding stone sill. The interstices are packed with *bouzillage,* the whole covered with stucco.

The outbuildings recently included a handsome

An old barn on the J. B. Vallé property was built in 1812 and blew down in the 1970s.

barn built in 1812 and a fine old smokehouse of hand-pressed brick. As late as 1966 there was still a ham hanging in there, shriveled to a tenth its orginal size. The old corn house, chicken house and milling shed are gone. And the barn, too is no more, flattened by a storm in the 1970s. It has been replaced by a modern structure, very similar in appearance to the original.

To the north is the old hickory Council Tree, said to be 250 to 300 years old. Vallé allegedly conducted numerous councils with the Indians beneath this tree. Reports that Pontiac was there probably are erroneous — the tree probably was there in the 1760s, but nothing else was. Pontiac was murdered in Cahokia in 1769.

The house now is occupied by Bernard K. Schram and his wife, the former Vion Papin. She is a great-granddaughter of Leon Vion. The building has been completely modernized and stands in eloquent testimony to the taste of the owners.

Bequette-Ribault House

West side of St. Marys Road,
½ mile south of South Gabouri Creek

This *poteaux en terre* house was built where it now stands by Jean Baptiste Bequette, possibly during the last quarter of the eighteenth century. Bequette, a *voyageur,* miller, and farmer, was married for the first time in 1778 to Louise LaCourse, second in 1786 to Celeste Truto and lastly in 1789 to Françoise Corset. Five of the six children born to these wives survived.

His descendants occupied the house until 1837 when it was acquired by "Clarise, a free woman of color." Clarise had been born in Virginia. She and her children by John Ribault, a wealthy French widower who came to Ste. Genevieve before 1819, lived in the house which was titled to her. Their descendants occupied the home until the death of their last grandson, Alonzo, in 1969.

The house possesses the classic shape of the Mississippi Valley creole architecture. It is constructed of red cedar logs placed vertically in a trench and hewn flat above grade. The roof is supported by Norman trusses of oak and rafters of peeled willow. *Bouzillage,* a mixture of clay and grass, fills the space between the logs and is smoothed over the logs both inside and out, like plaster. Whitewash of powdered lime and water is applied over the walls.

Now carefully restored by Royce and Margaret Wilhauk under the direction of architect Jack R. Luer and historic preservationist Jesse W. Francis, the house has returned to its original hip-roofed configuration. Missing side *galeries* have been replaced with

The excellent old Ribault house has been carefully restored by Royce and Margaret Wilhauk. It overlooks le grand champ.

assistance in determining the *galerie's* width by Melburn D. Thurman, Ph.D., archaeologist. The *galerie* ceiling was left open to facilitate air flow over the house, thus keeping it cooler in the days before fans and air conditioning. The house never had gas or running water.

Overby stated that two probate inventories generated at the deaths of Bequette's two wives, in 1786 and 1789, suggest the house was built not in 1770, as tradition has had it, but in 1789. Tree ring boring was done in 1985 and indicates that some of the trees were cut somewhat later, a

Top Photo:

The Ribault shutters, believed to be the originals, have tapered, dove-tailed battens fastened with wood pegs.

Bottom Photo:

The view beneath the front gallery of the Ribault reveals tunneling by wasps in the cedar logs of the poteaux en terre *construction.*

mystifiying situation at best. Knowledgeable architectural authorities, including Overby himself, were comfortable with 1789 as the date and are unable to explain the discrepancy.

In the restoration process, Francis used the same types of wood and the same kind of tools used by the original builder. He carefully matched the shutters to the three sets of originals found on the house. Local stone was used to rebuild the north fireplace, which had been partially removed.

The house is now open to the public as a living history museum. Visitors may participate, by appointment, in hearth cooking demonstrations and other activities.

Guibourd-Vallé House
Northwest corner, Fourth and Merchant streets

While the Bolduc is furnished in the manner of the typical middle-class French colonist, the Guibourd would appear to have been occupied by a nobleman. It was owned by Ann Vallé, who died in 1972. She was the widow of the great-great-great-grandson of François Vallé I, the first commandant of Ste.

The Guibourd-Vallé house

Genevieve, who in turn was the grandson of an early Quebec immigrant.

Mrs. Vallé maintained the home with great artistry and elegance. It had been near the point of no return in 1930, when her husband bought it and restored it to liveable condition. The garden to the rear and north sides of the home is one of the most meticulously cultivated in town. It is in bloom almost constantly in the growing season.

Jacques Guibourd is known to have acquired the title to the entire block through a grant from the Spanish government in 1799. The house, according to tree ring studies, evidently was built in 1806-07.

The gallery across the front of the Guibourd-Vallé house is entered from either end.

The rear gallery of the Guibourd-Vallé house has been glassed in with casement windows. It overlooks one of Ste. Genevieve's most handsome gardens.

It is characterized by a great gallery transversing the front, entered from either end. It has two front entrance doors, a feature that was not unique among French colonial homes. The door hardware is original — cast-iron lock sets with handles instead of knobs.

A brick kitchen was underneath the gallery. The

original walnut beams, with beaded edges, still support the ceiling.

The Guibourd holds the only remaining example of authentic original fenestration in Ste. Genevieve. The windows along the rear of the house proper, inside the sunporch, are twelve-lighted casements which swing in, and are believed to be original.

Rooms in the Guibourd-Vallé house are furnished to the taste of a French nobleman.

The great oak beams of the Guibourd-Vallé Norman truss are pegged in place.

The house was remodeled in the nineteenth century to conform to the American taste. The six-panel doors and their hardware date to this period. Evidently the interior hallway was created at that time. The height of the doorways indicate that all occupants of the house — through the remodeling period — were short in stature, a characteristic of the pioneer French.

Windows in the rear poteaux sur solle wall, overlooking the sun room, are inward-opening twelve-light casements, believed to be the original.

Of *poteaux sur solle* construction, the interstices between the great cedar logs are filled with plaster. In the attic is one of the town's finest examples of the Norman truss. The gables are punctuated by four windows — each glazed with the original water glass. The square nails penetrating the roof underlayment haven't begun to rust — there are no machine-made nails in the roof.

A complete guest house built about 1935 stands on the rear of the property. The former slave quarters are connected to the house proper.

Guibourd, a native of Angers, France, came to Santo Domingo as a secretary to a wealthy planter. He was saved during the bloody insurrection by a servant, Moros, who accompanied him to Ste. Geneviève. He became a wealthy farmer, tanner, and slave holder.

The house is owned by the Foundation for Restoration of Ste. Geneviève and is open daily. There is a small admission fee.

Janis-Ziegler House

(Green Tree Tavern)
St. Marys Road, just south of South Gabouri Creek

Nicholas Janis emigrated from Canada to Kaskaskia and married there in 1751. His son, François, is believed to have been the builder of the Janis-Ziegler house. François Janis was married at Prairie du Rocher in 1781 and moved shortly thereafter to Ste. Genevieve.

The house was built at the present site in 1791, according to the borings. It is the only house of this vintage utilizing an Anglo-American roof truss. The truss is not the original — the roof members were cut in 1808. The roof is supported by 150 young walnut trunks. The members are mortised and tenoned, with pegs used throughout.

The Janis-Ziegler house (Green Tree Tavern), with St. Marys road in the foreground

Round boxwood logs rest on a stone foundation three feet thick. The interstices are latticed with twigs, then filled with plaster. A kitchen of rose brick is under the north end of the west gallery. New Orleans style walnut shutters are said to bear their original stain — most certainly the hardware is original. The three-inch planked floors throughout the house are pegged.

The Janis-Ziegler is one of the few examples of Creole-French houses where the gallery girdles the entire frame, except for the kitchen which is placed underneath the gallery.

The great fireplace in the Janis-Ziegler house has three openings — this one into the living room, and one in each of two bedrooms behind it.

A great "coffin" door is used as a main entrance. Entryways in homes of this vintage often were larger than needed because funerals and wakes were conducted in the parlor, and the casket had to go through the door.

The house has a curious triangular fireplace, with openings in the parlor and in each of the two bedrooms behind the parlor. The configuration extends down into the earthen cellar. There is a hollow in the center of the fireplace foundation large enough for two or three people. A similar fireplace was in the other end of the building but no longer exists.

Janis converted the seventy-five foot by forty-five foot building into a tavern and boarding house immediately after 1804 to capitalize on the Louisiana Purchase. An early sign of the Green Tree Tavern — perhaps the original — is in the Ste. Genevieve Museum.

Shutters on the front wall of the Janis-Ziegler house are believed to have their original stain.

An English traveler, Thomas Ashe, mentioned the tavern in writings dated 1806:

> I heard the bells of the Catholic Church ring for vespers long before I entered the town. I did not wander from the peal but rode on with speed and animation, and put up at an inn which had strong indication of comfort. I was by no means disappointed; the landlord, a lively Frenchman, looked after my horses and his wife made me a cup of coffee with as much perfection as ever I drank at the *Palais Royal* or at the foot of *Pont Neuf*.

Janis owned a sugar mill on the Aux Vases. Sometime prior to 1833 the building was sold to Matthew Ziegler, who operated a tobacco store there for a number of years before it was converted to a residence. His great-grandson and namesake, owner of the Dufour, Shaw, and Fur Trading Post, retained an account book showing that whiskey cost forty cents a gallon— due to such a low bulk price, free snorts could be given to the customers.

There could be no truth to the rumor that the horses of the guests were sheltered under the rear gallery, unless the horses were three feet tall. It also is questionable that the building was ever in service as a fortification, as has been rumored.

Still, the joists supporting the rear gallery are notched in places, and could have accommodated ropes used in the operation of firing shutters. Since the stables definitely are known to have been to the rear of the property, and since the Osage were quite active during the fifteen year period after the house was erected, the installation of such devices would have made good sense.

The house currently is owned by Frankye Donze and usually is open to the public daily during the tourist season.

Shaw House
Southwest corner, Second and Merchant streets

Much has been learned about the Dr. Benjamin Shaw House since its purchase and management by the Missouri Department of Natural Resources.

The front two rooms were constructed by Jean Baptiste Bossier some time after he acquired the property from Parfait Dufour in November 1818. Bossier, a merchant, built the 20′ x 33′ building for his store and office. Silhouettes of the original counters and shelves ap-

The Mammy Shaw house

pear on the original painted wallboards.

Bossier sold the structure to Dr. Benjamin Shaw in 1837. Shaw, a widower, married Emelie Janis Lecompte in 1845 and added a room across the back and two more fireplaces in the house. The dividing wall between the front two rooms was moved to its present location and windows were added. The roofline was extended and two rooms were created above with a dormer added to the front. Shaw died March 12, 1849. Their only child, Marianne Joseph Shaw, was born three months later. "Mammy" Shaw con-

Emilie Shaw, who lived in the house from 1845 until her death fifty-two years later.

tinued to live in the house for the next forty-eight years, until her death in 1897 at age 90.

Three doors, supposedly from the pilot house of the *Dr. Franklin II,* separate the bedroom from the living room. An old cast iron coal-burning fireplace, said to have been on that boat, is in the bedroom. A fine ornamental cut glass door also came from the *Franklin.* Made by the firm of Curl-

The door hardware in Ste. Genevieve homes is most unusual. This lock is in the Shaw House.

ings and Robertson of Philadelphia, the door was dated by the manufacturer between 1834 and 1850.

The marks of the adz on the hand-hewn oak timbers supporting the ceiling still are very evident, as are the plane marks on the ceiling boards. Matthew E. Ziegler, who lived in the house until his death in 1980, added the entrance, which was common to the house and adjacent "Fur Trading Post."

Cut glass doors from the wreck of the old steamboat, Dr. Franklin II, *separate the bedroom from the living room of Shaw house. Some panes were left clear to provide visibility for the vessel's captain.*

"Fur Trading Post"

West side of Second Street, just south of Merchant

The "Fur Trading Post"

Keystone arch construction is seen in the old fireplace in the "slave quarters" section of "Fur Trading Post".

A huge fireplace in the upper level of the "Fur Trading Post" is decorated circa 1785.

Despite years of study by the former owner, the late Matthew E. Ziegler, the name of the builder of this structure, just to the rear of (and connected to) the Mammy Shaw house, is unknown. So is the date of its erection. Dr. Overby has concluded, however, that Parfait Dufour erected the structure as one of the buildings of the mill complex he operated on that lot. Ziegler, who was one of the area's best known artists, connected the two old buildings with a stone structure which served as his living quarters, gallery, and studio. A charming patio is between this building and the Shaw House.

The building had been unoccupied from 1900 to

about 1950.

The "Fur Trading Post" is now owned by the Department of Natural Resources of the State of Missouri.

Beauvais House

Southeast corner, Main and Merchant streets

While the outward appearance of this house has been subjected to extensive alterations, the ponderous cedar and walnut *poteaux en terre* frame still is substantially as it was in 1792, the year of its erection. (Tree ring studies show the north half of the house was added in 1800.)

It was built as a four-room house by Vital St. Gemme Beauvais. Henry M. Brackenridge, who lived there for several years as a young boy, indicated that it had galleries along the front and rear only. At that time a fireplace divided the house into two parts — one serving as a kitchen and the other serving as just about

The appearance of Beauvais house is greatly changed from the days when it was the home of Henry M. Brackenridge.

everything else — master bedroom, dining room, and parlor. Each of the areas had one bedroom to the rear. Like many other houses in Ste. Genevieve before 1800, it was surrounded with cedar pickets seven to eight feet high. A handsome old brick smokehouse to the rear, built in the early 1800s, still stands.

The house is smaller than when originally built. Overby discovered the side wall had been moved inward five feet, for reasons unknown today.

At one time a room to the north housed the first post office in Ste. Genevieve.

The log walls are filled with a *pierrotage* of stone and lime mortar. Some of the ancient walnut beams in the basement measure eighteen inches thick and were sagging badly, but since have been properly braced. Portions of the earthen cellar have been dug down for headroom, but all along the exterior walls the earth backfill comes to within a foot or two of the beams.

Great logs of poteaux en terre *construction penetrate the earth in the cellar of Beauvais. Note how the split walnut flooring planks are shaved to pass over the great beams.*

The split walnut flooring planks were notched in places where they pass over the great beams to provide a level floor above. The shutter hardware is believed to be original.

The house had a partial restoration by Frankye and Norbert Donze, who sold it to Al Keiser. He found a stone-lined well in the backyard. Jerry and Jackie Grindstaff later added a formal garden and operated the place as a tour house. It was purchased recently from the Grind-staff family and will be restored to its appearance in the late 1700s, as described by Henry Marie Brackenridge in his *Recollections of Persons and Places in the West.*

Jerry and Jackie Grindstaff installed a formal garden at the rear of the Beauvais house in 1987.

Memorial Cemetery
Fifth and Merchant streets

Despite periodic desecration by vandals, the old Ste. Genevieve cemetery remains one of the most pictur-esque sights in town. Here are buried the men and women who, two centuries ago, built the houses now bearing their names. Some of the stones carry birth dates from the early 1700s.

The casual visitor is often horrified at the sight of what are believed to be open graves. Many of those graves are in the New Orleans tradition — concrete enclosures perhaps two feet high, covered with a slab of concrete. Some of the walls are broken out and some of the capstones sag, revealing a void below.

Actually, the Ste. Genevieve pioneers were buried

The monument on the left marks the final resting place of Commandant and Mrs. J. B. Vallé, in Ste. Genevieve Memorial Cemetery. The Felix and Odile Vallé marker is at the far right.

six feet under — the style of marker is merely imitative of New Orleans. Still, the destruction — both from vandalism and natural causes — is deplorable. In the great Guibourd mausoleum, with its front a simulation of the slide-in, above-ground type of burial vault, a two-foot-square hole has been punched in the back elevation, revealing a hollow vault.

The first grave was that of Louis LeClere in 1796. Others include Ferdinand Rozier, J. B. Vallé, Guibourd, Senator Linn, Henri and François Janis, Vital St. Gemme Beauvais, Charles Gregoire, Col. Felix Vallé and his wife Odile Pratte Vallé, who was the last of the 3,000 to be interred there.

The cemetery is divided into three sections. The

south half, now completely filled, is Catholic. The northeastern quarter is reserved for Protestants, and the northwest corner for the Odd Fellows Lodge. It is in the Protestant section that twelve unidentified victims of the explosion of the *Dr. Franklin II* are buried.

The people of Ste. Genevieve have spent thousands of dollars of their own money and countless hours in restoration of the old cemetery. Lucille Basler and the Foundation for Restoration of Ste. Genevieve raised funds for that purpose. Basler did much of the restoration work personally.

The cemetery is open to the public during daylight hours throughout the year without charge.

Stone Icehouse

East side of alley paralleling and between Third and Fourth streets, midway between South Gabouri and Market streets.

Before the lot was excavated on the north side of this building, a high opening on that face was the same height off the terrain as the bed of a wagon. It probably was used for cold storage throughout its early life, as there is no evidence of a fireplace.

An opening in the gable of old stone icehouse probably was for an ice chute. The wood above the stone indicates the roof was raised sometime after its original construction.

The structure probably was built by J. B. Thomure shortly after 1800. A tunnel, built in 1904, connects the stone building to an old stable immediately to the east. Anna Thomure reports the tunnel was built after a disastrous fire as a refuge for the livestock. The walls of the icehouse are extremely thick, and no information exists as to why the roof was raised. It is not open to the public.

François Vallé II House
167 South Gabouri Street, between Main and Second

This is the house of the second Spanish civil commandant. The tree sudies indicates that the timbers were harvested in 1791.

François Vallé II was born in the Illinois country in 1758 and is known to have owned the entire west half of this block in 1790. He was appointed civil and

Only the poteaux sur solle *construction of the inner wall and the ceiling beams remain of this greatly altered house of François Vallé II.*

military commandant in 1783. By 1787 there were three houses on the lot. He had thirty-nine slaves, all of them believed to have been quartered on that property.

Adz marks still are visible in the overhead of the François Vallé II house, overlooking South Gabouri creek.

The house has been modernized to the point where it appears to have been built about 1895 or 1900. The old cedar logs making up the *poteaux sur solle* construction are visible beneath loose siding boards, however.

The old Norman truss is completely gone from the overhead. About all of the original that remains are the walls, foundation, and great walnut logs spanning sill to sill in the overhead. They still bear marks of the adz.

The building is a private residence not open to the public.

Price Brick Building

Northeast corner, Third and Market streets

The first brick building in Ste Genevieve, the Price Brick, now houses a Ste. Genevieve restaurant.

Built about 1804 by John Price, it was lost only sixteen years later when Sheriff Israel Dodge brought his hammer down to satisfy an indebtedness Price had incurred with a fellow citizen, Joseph Pratte.

Price was one of the first Americans in Ste. Genevieve. He moved there from Kentucky in 1789 to engage in trade with Louisville and Nashville. He was granted a six-year license to operate a ferry between Ste. Genevieve and Kaskaskia.

The handsome, handmade brick is laid up in a Flemish bond. Smaller brick in common bond at the gables indicates that the building probably had a hip roof at one time. The English influence is indicated by the dentil cornice.

There appears to be no foundation to the rumor that the brick for this building was bought to America from France as ballast for a sailing vessel. When the ships needed ballast it was generally provided in the form of slate. There were plenty of kilns downstream capable of such production, and there may even have

The Price Brick building is now a restaurant.

been one in Ste. Genevieve by that time.

The structure still has its original windows. It seems to have been built as a residence, although for a number of years it served as the first courthouse in Ste. Genevieve.

The Price Brick house is open to the public during the regular restaurant hours. There is no admission charge.

Linden House
East side of Main, between Market and South Gabouri streets

Early deed references indicate that this lot was sold by Jean Baptiste Moreau, Sr., to "Jemmien" (Gemien) Beauvais in 1811, and Beauvais evidently started construction of the Linden House shortly thereafter. There may have been a cabin on the site at the time of the sale. The house was enlarged after 1860 by Ludwina Wilder.

Originally the Linden was a two-room *poteaux sur solle* house with a relatively lightweight truss.

The late Constance A. and Harry B. Mathews, Jr., helped fund restoration of the Linden in 1959, which was directed by Dr. Ernest Allen Connally. The house now serves as headquarters for the National Society of Colonial Dames in America in the State of Missouri.

Dufour House
South side of Merchant Street, between Second and Third streets

Parfait Dufour bought this lot in 1793. His son Theophilus is known to have built this house in 1837, but he probably lived next door west. Parfait Dufour is said to have accompanied Col. George Rogers Clark in his march from Kaskaskia to Vincennes.

The Parfait Dufour House

A *poteaux en terre* cabin measuring ten feet by fifteen feet was known to have been on this site in early days, but there seems to be no trace of it now. Probably it was razed in the early 1800s to make room for this house, which is only slightly larger. The Dufour is of American frame construction, covered with lap siding. An enormous stone chimney, possibly the original, is along the rear of the house.

The Dufour is not open to the public.

Millard-Vallé House

1007 North Main, formerly Little Rock Road, about 1.5 miles north of North Gabouri Creek

This central-hall house was built with cut stone on the east and south faces, and fieldstone on the other walls. It was erected by Josiah Millard and purchased by Jean Baptiste Vallé as a residence for his son, François Vallé, and François's wife, Catherine Beauvais Vallé, Henry M. Brackenridge's "Zouzou." It has ten fireplaces and is little changed from the original configuration. Restored by Frank and Shirley Myers, the house is not open to the public.

The Millard-Vallé House

LaLumendière House
801 South Gabouri

François Moreau is known to have obtained from the Spanish a land grant of substantial acreage along the South Gabouri. He sold a lot on the property to Antoine LaLumendière, who built this house on the site in about 1800-05. It remained in that family until 1959. It is a single story, *poteaux sur solle* building.

The LaLumeundiére house

and was saved from destruction by the Foundation for Restoration of Ste. Genevieve. The house has since been sold to James LaLumendiére and is slated for restoration soon. It is not open to the public.

Ste. Genevieve Catholic Church

Southwest corner, Dubourg Place and Merchant Street

This towering, Gothic Revival church, built between 1876 and 1880, stands on the same tract that was the site of the first church in the new town. That old log church was moved to the high ground in 1794. A stone

The old stone church, built on the present church property during the 1830s

The present Victorian-Gothic church

The Catholic church nave

church consecrated in 1837 served until the late 1870s.

The foundations of both the stone and log churches are still visible in the basement of the present edifice.

The first log church is believed to have been built on *le grand champ* in 1754. There were plans for a new church to replace it, but no proof

Commandant and Madame François Vallé II are buried beneath this plaque in front of the church nave.

exists that the old log church wasn't the same one which was moved up to the new town. It was erected by Philibert Watrin, S.J., cure of Kaskaskia and named St. Joachim.

Commandant and Madame François Vallé II, Father James Maxwell, Rev. Henri Pratte and François Corset, the "chantre," are buried beneath the nave of the church.

The impact of the French in the congregation was

felt for a long time. As late as 1890 the church was being served by an old French bedeau, Papa Girard. He would awaken sleepers by a vigorous nudge of the collection box. Those who made liberal contributions were met with a bow and an offer of snuff.

Linn House

North side of Merchant Street, just west of Second Street

The Linn house, built in 1806, is important as much for the prominence of its owner as for its age. The two-story frame building, modified extensively, has a roofline suggestive of the saltbox houses of New England.

Dr. Lewis F. Linn was one of the most noted early senators. By encouraging settlement of the Pacific Northwest, Senator Linn laid the groundwork for a favorable compromise with England over the establishment of the border between Canada and the Oregon Territory.

Linn moved to Ste. Genevieve to pratice medicine in 1816 and served in the senate from 1833 to 1843. He died in Ste. Genevieve while treating victims of a cholera epidemic.

His house was built by Abraham Newfield and sold in 1820 to Ferdinand Rozier. Linn bought it in 1826 and lived there until 1837.

The home of Lewis F. Linn, the "Model Senator from Missouri"

The house is not open to the public.

Dufour-Rozier Building
Northwest corner, Second and Merchant streets

This two-story cut stone structure is believed to have been built by the trading firm of Keil, Bisch, and Roberts in 1818 as an office/warehouse. It was sold in 1831 to Senator Lewis F. Linn. It is now occupied by a printing company.

The Dufour-Rozier building

Felix Vallé House
Southeast corner, Second and Merchant streets

This one and one-half-story ashlar stone structure was built in the Federal style in 1818 by a Ste.

The Felix Vallé house

Genevieve merchant, Jacob Philipson. It was purchased in 1824 by J. B. Vallé after Philipson moved with his family to Old Mines, Missouri. Felix Vallé, the fourth son of J. B. Vallé, bought it from his father in 1835 and lived in the home until his death in 1877. The home was acquired by the Missouri Department of Natural Resources several years ago.

That agency carefully restored the structure to its configuration during the years it served both as a home and a place of business for Felix and his wife Odile Pratte. The commercial side of the home was occupied by the trade firm of Menard & Vallé and their store has been authentically recreated by the present owners.

The home retains much of its original interior woodwork as well as an elaborate denticulated front cornice. To the rear of the home stand two outbuildings believed to have been built by Valle after he occupied the home.

The house is now open to the public daily as a state historic site. There is a small admission charge.

Hubardeau House
Northeast corner, Fourth and Jefferson streets

Records exist showing that Simon Hubardeau ordered glass for a new house in 1769—obviously for a building he was erecting on *le grand champ*. This building, built by J. Bte. Hubardeau, was here in 1817. The two-story house is somewhat modified from the original configuration.

The building contains its original floors, supported by adzed log joists. The windows have all been replaced by modernized designs. A doorway on the Fourth Street side was filled with stone to match the balance of the west facade.

A one-story brick addition was added about the time of the Civil War. The house is not open to the public.

A doorway once occupied the blank space near a corner of the Hubardeau House. A brick addition, built at the time of the Civil War, is at left.

Bolduc-LeMeilleur House
Southwest corner, Main and Market streets

This building was purchased in 1966 with the aid of a gift from the late Constance A. and Harry B. Mathews, Jr. It was in an advanced state of disrepair— a second-story porch was sagging and ready to fall.

The building was then restored as a one and one-half-story structure, believed by some to be its original configuration. An old brick building to the north was removed to expose the north elevation to the public.

Ernest Allen Connally directed the restoration of the house.

Etienne Bolduc, Louis's son, married Catherine Janis on August 1, 1792, and some authorities interpret Louis's will to indicate that a two-story frame house was on the site at that time. A brick store was built on the corner in 1820.

When Louis died in November 1815 a sale was held and this portion of his lot was bought by Catherine Janis Bolduc, by then a widow.

Her daughter, Agathe, married René Lemeillure in 1815, and apparently they all lived there together after the house was built, probably in 1820. Both René and Agathe died before Catherine, who sold the property to the Sisters of Loretto in 1837. At the same time, the sisters received the little brick building on the corner from J. B. Vallé. The structures stood about ten feet apart and were connected by a wooden passage. Eleven years later the sisters sold the combined property, which then became the Detchmendy Hotel.

Connally believes it was this owner who raised the Bolduc-LeMeilleur to a two-story structure, but many others feel the two-story building, which supposedly was erected in 1792, and the two-story building converted to a one and one-half story home in 1968, were one and the same.

The interior was furnished as a memorial to Mrs. Mathews. It is occasionally opened to the public.

The Bolduc-LeMeilleur house underwent extensive restoration. It was returned to a one-and-one-half-story configuration.

Ste. Genevieve Academy
Northwest corner, Fifth and Washington streets

This two-story stone building was built in the Federal style in 1808 and used as a school for boys intermittently from 1810 until the Civil War period, when it was closed.

Owned by the Ste. Genevieve School District, it was reconditioned to serve as an educational facility for special children. The Ste. Genevieve Foundation restored the old building but has failed to find a suitable use for it. It is gradually deteriorating, and is not often open to visitors.

The old Ste. Genevieve Academy is a handsome building to-day, 160 years after it was built.

Ratte-Hoffman House
Southeast corner, Main and South Gabouri streets

This great two-story frame building is sited on an eminence overlooking the South Gabouri Creek, and if something isn't done soon it's going to fall into it. The core of the building measures about twenty-six feet by seventeen feet, and brick chimneys flank the side elevations. It was built in 1809. The house, black from lack of paint, is not open to the public.

The decaying Ratte-Hoffman house towers above eminence on South Gabouri Creek.

The old two-story Ratte-Hoffman home is now occupied by a junk dealer. The porches are sinking from the core of the house.

Inn St. Gemme Beauvais

Main and Jefferson streets

This structure, the fifth historic building restored by Frankye and Norbert Donze, was built in 1849 by Felix Rozier. Prior to that time the land was the barn lot of Vital St. Gemme Beauvais. The home was sold in 1923 to Lawrence Donze, who sold it to his son, Norbert, in 1948. Due to many articles in books and magazines, it has become one of the best known bed-and-breakfast inns in the Midwest.

It is now operated by Paul Swenson and Marcia

The Inn St. Gemme Beauvais

Willson, and is gaining a reputation for fine cuisine. Reservations: (314) 883-5744.

Southern Hotel

Third and Market streets

The so-called John Donohue home is believed to have been erected in 1820 and modernized twice during the rest of that century. It has a "grandma's cooler" atop the building, a natural air conditioner which cools today through air convection.

The present owners, Barbara and Mike Hankins, have concluded an extensive restoration program and now operate another of Ste. Genevieve's quality bed-and-breakfast inns. They have challenged the 1820 dating of the house, and feel at least part of the building was there in 1804. That was when the widow of François Vallé II sold the property.

Reservations: (314) 883-3493.

The Southern Hotel

There are a number of other notable houses in old Ste. Genevieve. There is the so-called Winston cabin, believed to be enclosed in a fairly new house at 186 South Seventh Street. There is the Larose cabin, on out the South Gabouri, and a small log house two blocks due west of the Winston place. There is a fine old Greek Revival house standing across from the church on Third Street, built about 1830 by Charles Gregoire.

There probably are a dozen or so old log cabins buried inside homes that even the owners don't know about. For example, in 1967 a house was demolished on the northeast corner of North Third and Jefferson streets—inside was a two-room *poteaux sur solle* cabin. There are one or two outbuildings of horizontal log construction still standing in the upper part of town.

Remains of a two-room vertical log cabin were recently torn down at North Third and Jefferson streets.

In the north end of town are two buildings now nearing 200 years of age. The Louis Caron and Antoine Aubuchon houses now appear as fairly contemporary structures.

Ste. Genevieve seems to be growing in awareness of the need to preserve its old buildings. The remains of the cabin mentioned above were salvaged by Frankye and the late Norbert Donze, who contemplated rebuilding it at another location.

But you can't win 'em all. Only a few years ago the splendid old Misplait house, which stood just north of the Amoureux and was believed to have been one of the survivors of the flood of 1785, had fallen victim to such negligence that it had to be torn down. Even the stone well, with the typical French tent roof over its windlass had been filled in.

Moses Austin sold some ground after he left Ste. Genevieve which, according to the deed, was improved with a fine brick mansion. It was demolished in the nineteenth century.

But one of the Austin outbuildings survives, numbered 72 South Gabouri Street. It was purchased

The Moses Austin outbuilding

in 1987 by the Ste. Genevieve Jour de Fete Committee with profits from their annual celebration and is expected to be restored in future years. The southern portion of the building is believed to have been built in 1810; the northern portion several decades later.

One visit well worth the effort and small cost is to the Ste. Genevieve Museum, on the southeast corner of

The Ste. Genevieve Museum, on the town square, houses many objects of interest to tourists.

Dubourg and Merchant streets. The building, erected in 1935, contains much memorabilia of the past, with concentration on the mid-nineteenth century. One notable exception is an intact salt evaporating bowl found at the Saline Spring. Also on display is an original watercolor by Audubon and the original wood sign from the Green Tree Tavern. There also are a number of sights worth seeing around Ste. Genevieve. One of the most picturesque is the Vallé Spring, site of the mammoth bicentennial program in 1935. It is reached by taking Fourth Street out to where it branches with Cemetery Road, then across U.S. 61 about a half-mile. Just before the road forks to go to the "new" cemetery, a

The outflow from Vallé Spring was dammed in 1935 to create a miniature Mississippi River, a prop for the town's bicentennial celebration.

The Saline Spring is now just a patch of muddy ground and a puddle.

a trail leads to the left and down into the spring.

The "new" cemetery itself absorbs many hours of Ste. Genevieve visitors. There are great old names here too. Some bodies were removed from their graves in the old cemetery just after the new one was opened, including that of Louis Bolduc.

A visit to the famous Saline Spring may prove a bit disappointing. Now it is just a patch of muddy ground with a trickle of mildly saline water oozing from it here and there. Two centuries ago, it was the heart and cause of a thriving settlement. In recent years archaeologists have uncovered treasures many hundreds of years old, reminders of the great Mississippian civilizations that worked there. The site of the Kreilich excavations is at the near edge of a field just beyond the spring itself.

Saline Spring is reached by taking U.S. 61 south six miles to the bridge over Saline Creek. A few feet north

The Burnt Mill now is a grotesque ruin on the banks of Saline Creek.

of the bridge, turn west onto "J." About two-tenths of a mile up the road is a marker for an underground telephone cable crossing. Follow the crossing south about fifty yards to a bare, muddy area about fifty feet wide and one hundred feet long. That's the Saline Spring.

A far richer experience awaits anyone willing to drive the twenty miles to the Burnt Mill. This is a great stone structure on the banks of the Saline, just inside the Perry County line.

François Vallé II built the mill in 1800 along the Three-Notch Road from Mine La Motte, where the old lead roads ford the Saline. It burned during the Civil War, and charred remains of its beams may be seen in the notches in the stone walls.

A view from the bridge over the Saline creek in Perry County shows the power of the forest to conceal the Burnt Mill.

The Burnt Mill ruin, although sixty-five feet high, is about to be engulfed by foliage.

In the wintertime the great stone ruin towers in plain view, some sixty-five feet over the bank of the Saline. In summer it is nearly obscured by the foliage, despite the fact that it is no more than fifteen yards from the bank of the creek.

The mill may be reached by taking U.S. 61 fifteen miles south to where Highway NN branches off to the right, about one mile north of Brewer. Follow NN three and one-half miles. Turn south on a hard surface road and go perhaps one-tenth mile — a bridge is there at the bottom of a steep hill. Stop on the bridge and look to the right. The sight is staggering.

There are two attractions of great magnitude in Illinois near Ste. Genevieve. Both Kaskaskia and Fort de Chartres are shrouded in memories of tragedy.

Kaskaskia was founded in 1703 along the west bank of the Kaskaskia River, about four miles upstream from the Mississippi. At first there were only the Jesuit Gabriel Marest, Chief Rouensa and his Kaskaskia Indians, a few Frenchmen, and the remainder of the Tamaroa who elected to abandon Cahokia to gain some relief from the marauding Sioux.

At the new site they were joined by a number of French traders. By 1707 the population had grown to 2,200 and continued to grow substantially for the next several decades.

The Jesuits saw to it that one of the first buildings on the site was a church — the mission church of the Immaculate Conception. Built in 1703 of logs, it soon proved too small for the rapidly-growing town. In 1740 a new stone church was placed in use. A third church was made of vertical logs in 1775 but was pulled down in 1838 because of its deterioration. The final church, of brick, was built in 1838

This early drawing is of Kaskaskia in its prime.

The cornerstone of the church of 1737, with the date still legible, was remounted in the building constructed to house the ''Liberty Bell of the West,'' on Kaskaskia Island.

The old altar, carved by hand from walnut for the church of 1737, now is in the sacristy of the Church of the Immaculate Conception, Kaskaskia Island.

and still serves the Kaskaskians, although now in a different location.

In 1718 Pierre Duque de Boisbriant became commandant of the Illinois country and moved from New Orleans to Kaskaskia with a great number of the military. While the officers and men were housed in town, Boisbriant and a contingent of workmen built Fort de Chartes along the Mississippi, some sixteen miles north of Kaskaskia.

The presence of the military caused considerable crowding in the town, and in 1719 the Indians were ordered out. They founded the so-called Indian Kaskaskia about five miles up the Kaskaskia River from town.

As the French began to traffic more and more in the Middle Valley, the fame of Kaskaskia spread to Europe. Word of the town reached Versailles, and Louis XV presented Kaskaskia with a 650-pound bronze bell cast in 1741. The bell now is enshrined in

Kaskaskia's "Liberty Bell of the West"

the Fort Kaskaskia Memorial Building on Kaskaskia Island.

It was this old town that received George Rogers Clark and the cause of the American Revolution the night of July 4, 1778, and it was this same bell that called the people to hear Pierre Gibault's plea for acquiescence. It is eleven years older than the Liberty Bell in Independence Hall. Around its upper rim it bears the legend, in French: "For the Church of the Illinois, with the compliments of the King from beyond the sea."

The bell was retired by a carillon of new bells in 1873 and stored in an old building. A flood crumpled the structure, and it wasn't until 1918 that the bell was recovered and brought to the island.

When old Kaskaskia was founded on the west bank of the Kaskaskia River, the Mississippi was about two miles to the west. The stretch between the two rivers

Top Map:

In 1880 the Mississippi River swung dangerously close to the old town of Kaskaskia, located on the southwest bank of the Kaskaskia river. The two-mile distance between the two rivers had narrowed to 400 feet by 1880

Lower Map:

By 1915 the devastation which started with the flood of 1881 was complete, and the old town site was in the center of the Mississippi channel. Survivors relocated in Ste. Genevieve and in the center of the peninsula.

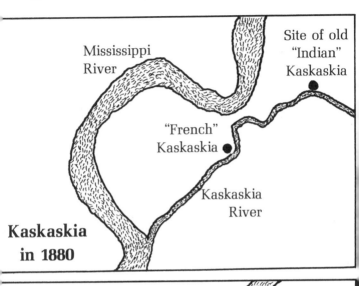

Mississippi River

Site of old "Indian" Kaskaskia

"French" Kaskaskia

Kaskaskia River

Kaskaskia in 1880

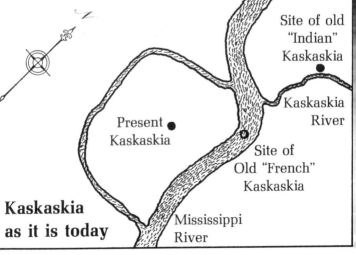

Site of old "Indian" Kaskaskia

Kaskaskia River

Present Kaskaskia

Site of Old "French" Kaskaskia

Kaskaskia as it is today

Mississippi River

was alluvium and subject to continuing erosion and inundation.

In 1844 the Mississippi boiled out of its banks, but it didn't reach Kaskaskia. It did cause the Kaskaskia River to back up to the point where its waters were eight feet deep in the streets.

By 1881 the Mississippi had come within 400 feet of the Kaskaskia River. The little town was caught in a squeeze. In April of that year the Mississippi broke through just above Kaskaskia. The bed of the little river wasn't large enough to hold a fraction of the Mississippi's current, and the flooding was total. The Mississippi all but abandoned its loop around the old town, and the new channel went down the Kaskaskia. Within a few years the inhabitants of old Kaskaskia had gone to the high ground in the middle of the peninsula — their old homes were permanently beneath the Mississippi.

Old residents can recall rowing over the site of the old town and seeing chimneys and other stone structures still standing beneath the muddy waters.

Kaskaskia is reached today by traveling nine miles south on U.S. 61 to St. Marys, then turning east on Highway U. Just outside St. Marys is a long bridge which goes over a wide, flat cornfield several feet below. That cornfield used to be the Mississippi River.

The Church of the Immaculate Conception — the mission started by Father Marquette in 1675, when Kaskaskia was at Starved Rock in northern Illinois — is now in the center of Kaskaskia Island. It houses the hand-carved walnut altar built for the second church in 1738.

Next to the church is the shrine holding the old bell. Its cornerstone is the same one used for the old rock church, and the date of 1737 still is clearly visible.

Boisbriant evidently was a stranger to the ways of the Mississippi, for he built his Fort de Chartes right on the banks. It was hefty enough for Indians or British — a stout wood stockade reinforced on the interior with earth from the moat excavation. It was completed in 1720, but had to be rebuilt only seven years later.

The main gate at Fort de Chartres has been restored. The structure holds a cannon platform.

By 1732 the rebuilt fort was in such dilapidated shape from the poundings of the Mississippi that a new one was built upon higher ground. It soon fell into general disrepair also.

This is one of several buildings restored at Fort de Chartres. The portion at left served as a chapel for the troops.

In 1751, when the French apprehension over the English was running high, it was decided to build a more permanent fortification. A stone fort was started from plans drawn by François Saucier. In 1756, after three years of construction, the stone fort was completed.

The walls were eighteen feet high and two feet thick, enclosing four acres of buildings and parade grounds. The main gateway mounted a cannon platform. Included in the complex were a two-story building, guard house, chapel, government house, coach house, pigeon house, two buildings for officers' quarters, two long barracks, a massive powder magazine, kitchen and bake ovens, and four prison cells. It was described by a British officer as "the most commodious and best built fort in North America."

This huge powder magazine restored at Fort de Chartres has side walls five feet thick and end walls three feet thick.

For all of this, the fort served the French only eight years. The Treaty of Paris passed the lands east of the Mississippi to the English in 1763. They abandoned and destroyed the fort in 1772.

The state of Illinois has uncovered most of the breastworks and reconstructed a number of the old buildings. The Fort de Chartes State Park is open daily to the public without charge.

The most enjoyable way to reach the fort is to drive up North Main Street three miles from Ste. Genevieve to Little Rock Landing, board the automobile ferry there, and go across the Mississippi to the Modoc landing. However, the ferry changes hands frequently, and may not be running from time to time. A check with the Ste. Genevieve Tourist Information Center, (314) 883-5750, might be in order.

From the ferry landing in Illinois, follow the signs about three miles to Modoc, turn and head north four miles to Prairie du Rocher, then turn left on highway 155 to Fort de Chartes.

Appendix 2

The Nicknames of
Ste. Genevieve
Lorraine Stange

The following is the text of an address delivered before a meeting of the Foundation for Restoration of Ste. Genevieve on July 20, 1984, by Lorraine Stange, now the manager of the Bolduc House.

It was universally admired; therefore, it has been included in the fourth edition of this book.

I was recently approached with a rather interesting proposal — that of researching Ste. Genevieve nicknames. After mulling the idea over a bit, I began what I felt would be a rather limited project. Two years later I have yet to complete what has proved to be an enjoyable and fascinating venture.

Before sharing with you a limited selection of names, it is fitting that an explanation be offered as to why such an area lends itself to, and is worthy of, research.

For years visitors to Ste. Genevieve have commented on the seeming universality of nicknames in and among our local citizenry. Often times we hear, ''I've never been in a community where so many people are known and recognized by their nicknames.''

Look around. You probably live next door to someone who possesses a well-known nickname. Possibly a work acquaintance is known to you by such.

This phenomenon is so ingrained that morticians and sometimes families have to search baptismal records for proper names of individuals identified throughout life by a sobriquet acquired in childhood.

Contrary to popular belief, such a custom did not originate in the twentieth century. Recent research has revealed the incidence of nicknames among the eighteenth century French colonial settlers of Ste. Genevieve.

Louis Houck's *History of Missouri* mentions a number of nicknames from the eighteenth century, while Gregory Franzwa's *The Story of Old Ste. Genevieve,* includes sobriquets popular in the twentieth century.

W. A. Dorrance states in *The Survival of French in the Old District of Sainte Genevieve,* ''The creoles have retained the mania for grotesque nicknames and abbreviations for individuals or place names which excited such mirth among first Americans. As for personal nicknames their use was so popular that the practice remains in full vigor today. In Ste. Genevieve as in Old Mines the nickname of the father is inherited by his children.''

Archival records repeatedly carried the notation *dit,* meaning ''called,'' to identify *habitants* through their familiarly used nicknames. The persistence of this custom for more than two centuries changed radically through the first Anglo-American settlement after the 1804 Louisiana Purchase and the heavy mid-nineteenth century German influx. A major difference exists in the custom of selecting nicknames.

The eighteenth century settler was given a sobriquet for his surname; the contemporary practice lends itself to replacing first names with nicknames.

In providing the reader with this preliminary study, I have utilized the following sources, the Ste. Genevieve archives, dating from the 1750s; a variety of sources authored by Louis Houck, Gregory Franzwa, W. A. Dorrance, as well as Ferdinand Rozier; and interviews with the local residents. My mother, Vergi Stange, is extremely well-versed in this area and provided me with a large portion of contemporary nicknames. There remain many resources yet to be explored, and consequently, I offer only a limited amount of information on the subject of sobriquets.

It is my hope that with the completion of this research, consisting of a combination of documentary and oral resources, a unique and enlightening sidelight of local history can be gleaned to add to the knowledge of a community that has the reputation of being a unique entity.

In preparing this presentation I have questioned myself thus: "Should I make it safe and risk being a real drag, or should I tell everything, making it interesting and colorful and then engage legal counsel?" It is at this point my good friend Stanley Drury comes to mind, for he has supplied me with such choice nicknames, only to add, "Don't you dare use this one in print." It is my sincere hope that before I have set my research to rest that dear Stan will bring me some labels that *are* "fit to print."

Of course I could do as Gregory Franzwa so wisely did in *The Story of Old Ste. Genevieve:* present some of the more picaresque ones *en français.*

Let us begin with names that appear in the archival

records. I have found over 100 families listed who had
nicknames for the surname. That number is increased
manyfold since several family members share the same
sobriquet.

As often happens in historical documents such as
these dating from the 1750s, one encounters numerous
discrepancies such as the following example.

There appears a record of a *habitant* Bideau *dit*
Lapin, Pierre. Next we find Lapin *dit* Bideau, and yet
another entry reads Pidault *dit* Lapin, Pierre. Such
entries lead one to question which is the nickname and
which is the real name. Since Pierre Lapin translates to
Peter Rabbit, one could be fairly safe in assuming
Lapin as the sobriquet. And yet another contradiction
is that of LaChance *dit* Pepin and Pepin *dit* LaChance.
There also appears Maurice *dit* Chatillon as well as
Chatillon *dit* Maurice.

A number of nicknames reveal a bit of the personali-
ty of these French *habitants*. We find such entries as
Billeron *dit* La Fatique (the tired one), Billet *dit*
Beausoleil, Pierre (beautiful sunshine), Catout *dit* Brin
d'Amour (a bit of love), Chauvin *dit* Joyeuse (happy),
Courtois *dit* La Beau (the handsome one) — my junior
high students would take the liberty to translate this as
"the hunk" — Pepin *dit* LaChance (the lucky one),
Thibault *dit* Sans Chagrin (carefree), and Louvien *dit*
D'Amour (some love).

Some nicknames reveal the locale from whence the
settler came. We are introduced to Martin *dit* Cana-
dien, Azau *dit* Breton, Yvon and Ivon *dit* Versailles,
and Jean, Jolin, and Laulin *dit* La Rochelle, Jean.

The nickname *La Fleur* (the flower) appears as a
nickname for Louis Lambert in addition to that of
François Lalumondier and lastly as a sobriquet for

Joseph Peredat, Armand *dit* Sans Facon, Celeste (without ceremony), and lastly Herbert *dit* Le Conte (the falsehood). One of the more interesting findings for me personally was the entry of Louis LaCroix *dit* Seraphin selling a parcel of property to Joseph Germain. I was born in the Joseph Seraphin House, a vertical log structure dating from 1790. It remained in our family for fifty-two years, until it was sold in 1983. Seraphin surfaces again as a nickname for Ambrose Selequin. We find in the archives the really bizarre entry Pierre La Perle *dit* Janvier (Peter January). Some of these nineteenth century names have completely disappeared. However, the names Seraphin, La Fleur, and La Chance are very much in evidence today, as is La Rose, which is recorded as a sobriquet for André Deguire. The name Deguire is presently found in the Lead Belt area — how interesting that it is the nickname La Rose that remained with us.

In Houck's *History of Missouri* we meet Pierre Gautier *dit* Sans Quartier, Tessero, Gregoire *dit* Bebe, Olivier *dit* Belle Peche and, lastly, the strong and macho Nicolos Beaugenou *dit* Fifi.

The custom of nicknames, as was stated earlier, is very commonplace today in Ste. Genevieve. In glancing through the phone book one reads Popeye Eisenbis, Butts Scherer, Schnay Basler, Nip Roth, Cricket Dallas and Bossy Scherer.

Family nicknames appear on license plates, mailboxes, truck doors, and even gravestones. A contemporary innovation is the appearance of a nickname on the bugscreen of one's 4X4 pickup. The 200-year-old custom with a modern twist is alive and well in Ste. Genevieve.

A vast number in this French community, inhabited

by Germans, are known only by their sobriquets, whether it be Frenchy La Rose or Germany Jokerst. The proper name often times is recalled only after much thought, and sometimes not at all. It would be difficult to identify which Ron Roth we refer to, yet everyone knows Sleeper Roth.

Over many months of gathering data I have concluded the best known nickname to be that of Chicken . . . (*merde*). In my many interviews it was always the first mentioned. Only once did I encounter anyone who could tell me the gentleman's name was William.

We in Ste. Genevieve have that name in degrees, so to speak; positive comparative, and superlative — Chick Griffard, Chickie Burgess, and Chicken . . . Labruyère.

Rather than simply compiling a list of Who's Whom in Ste. Genevieve, I have attemped to present selected names via categories. Yet the categories seem endless — families, animals, insects, flowers, anatomical parts (a category that covers a multitude of sins), character traits, physical appearances. I have decided to share with you only the classics — those that have stood the test of time.

Family nicknames — why not start with the Donzes? How about those three brothers, Raymond, Marion, and Leo, known as Izzy, Dizzy, and Nuts. In my meetings with Izzy, who assisted me in this project, I was surprised to learn Izzy was a nickname for another nickname. As an elementary student our friend was dubbed Hebrew the Wind Away. When asked how such a name was born, Izzy remembered, ''I could run faster than any kid in school and I guess they thought I deserved it.''

Additional family members include cousins Boatsie and Batesie, Nooney, Cap, and Goofie. In any circle those names have to be regarded as prize winners.

The Sexauer family can also boast sobriquets of creativity. Enter the brothers — Guinea, Sleepy, Funny, Beans, Grampa, and Uncle Spot. The Weilers — you know Hoot-Owl, Jimbo, and Chico. The La Roses, labeled Sparrow, Dudley, Cocky, and Few Clothes, who earned his name in the following manner. As a young man La Rose sought employment as a river hand. When signing his name on the register (hoping to be hired that day he quite naturally brought a valise with him), a wind blew his bag completely off the table causing the comment, "You must have damn few clothes in there if the wind blew it away that easily." *Viola!* A legend was born.

The Basler family is also known by familiar sobriquets. Everyone in town knows Punkin and Chipper. Agnes Basler, widow of Leo (Punkin), related to me that when she and Leo were married she did not want to be known as Mrs. Punkin Basler. However, there were several Leo Baslers in town so she could not completely escape her husband's sobriquet. "I even introduced myself as Mrs. Leo C. Basler," she added, "but that did not help much." It was at that point Agnes decided it would not be passed on to their son. Upon his birth she gave him the name Chipper. Not because the boy is a "chip off the old block," as I had thought, but because the nurse found him to be a frisky, chipper little baby boy. To that Basler crew we add Beck, Big Foot, Little Big Foot, Batch, Moosey, Porky, and Schnay.

The circumstances of Ray Basler becoming Schnay are already known to several — this will make it known to even more. As a young lad Ray had quite a talent for snow script, or possibly it was good enough to be called "snow calligraphy." On snowy days when playing outdoors if our Ray needed to relieve himself, he simply spelled relief R-A-Y in the snow. I leave to the reader's imagination what he used for a pen. The Staab boys, neighbors to the Baslers, and knowing the German word for snow to be *schnay,* made our Ray infamous.

The Scherers for years have been our friends as Kee-Kee, Poogie, Piggy, Butts, and Hammer. In my conversation with Warren "Bossy" Scherer I related that Ken Rehm informed me Bossy was also known as Goo-Goo Eyes. Bossy's retort was, "Yeah, that sounds like something Flower Pot would say." (Ken "Flower Pot" Rehm is our local florist).

Time to move on to another category — animals — probably the most numerous of all, with hardly a creature being omitted. To the aforementioned Guinea and Piggy I offer you all those known as Goose, so many they truly constitute a gaggle of geese. We find them in the families of Schmelze, Giesler, Kraenzle, and Winston. Let me put to rest the idea that the name Goose came from a pinch on the derriere. In the Giesler family August, the father, was pronounced with a German accent, and through the years the term Goose was used in place of Ow-Goost!

We must include in this animal category brothers Mouse and Rat Schwent, as well as Moose Jokerst, Snakes Grass, Horse Morice, Hippo Sadler, the Toads — Grieshaber and Singley, Squirrel Irlbeck, Catfish Rottler and Wonder Warthog Kertz.

Being a town of 250 birthdays we are not without an assortment of Termites, Cockroaches, and Ants — the latter of which is preceded by a very descriptive four letter word.

Earlier I made mention of the creole custom of selecting names bordering on the grotesque. The practice is still prevalent today and consists largely of names I have placed in my ''unmentionables'' file. That list, however, is growing quite rapidly. The following, although a bit uncomplimentary, were and are commonly used today — Froggie K. because of numerous warts, Bat-Eye Arnold who had a ''bad'' eye, Sink Hole because of his alcohol consumption, and Black Root Bleckler.

My purpose is not to embarrass or offend anyone, and I certainly would not want to arouse the ire of any of Ste. Gen's toughest. Knock-Out Vineyard is known as such for his ability to start fights, Crusher Vaeth, Tuffy Howard, Zombie, Two-Gun Govereau, Killer Brown, our own Jack Dempsey, and Tarzan Arnold.

Paul Morice was very helpful in supplying me with information about nicknames, yet he was at a loss to tell me how brother Felix came to be known as Pecan. ''I don't know about Pecan,'' he said, ''but I'll tell you how Oscar Arnold earned the name of Tarzan. As kids we use to play down on the Gabouri Creek bank across from the Ziegler maids. At that time the whole area was more like a jungle of trees, brush, and vines. Ol' Oscar would swing from tree to tree with such skill we just called him Tarzan.''

To balance out all these tough guys, there were plenty of peacemakers, or so their names imply. Who could not get along with the likes of Smiley Taylor, Honey Wehner, Sweet Pea Vaeth, Pansy Herzog, Fluff Martin, Peaches Vaeth, Powder Buff, Funny Meyer and daughter Wee-Wee?

My next collection just seems to go together. Mr. Shuh is known as Foot Shuh. There, too, we find, Crabby Crass, Candy Bahr, and Fish Huck.

There are names that rhyme — Turkey Lurk, Izzy and Dizzy, and Jo-Ko La Plante.

Some are alliterative — Stringer Straughn, Shrimp Stanton, Dirty Donze, Nickelsplitter Naeger, and Roach Roth.

We have our famous pairs: father and son Moonie and Spider Okenfuss, husband and wife Icky and Duck Kreitler, businessmen Myron "Bones" Savage, and Stan "Droopy" Drury, and the administrators where I teach are Snookie Wilson and Flipper Miget.

I must admit my account has barely unearthed the colorful topsoil of Ste. Genevieve's garden of unique nicknames. There are many more sobriquets that need to be recorded. The stories behind the names also merit recording, for they, too, are a part of local history.

I shall conclude by saying we have everything from A to Z in Ste. Genevieve. Apple-Knocker Schwent, Bots Greishaber, Chevy-Jose Gendron, Do-Do Wehner, Ernie Schmelze, Flakes Bahr, Gump Roth, High Pockets Kreitler, Itchy Rudloff, Jazbo Scherer, Kilowatt Gegg, Lemon Klein, Moon Williams, Nooks Oberle, Ockie Giesler, Peck Wehner, Quickstart, Ratsy Behr, Snew Fallert, Toothpick Bollinger Ugh Wilson, Waddle Schmelze, Yitty Wehmeyer, and Zombie.

Bibliography

Alvord, Clarence W. *The Illinois Country 1673-1818.*
  Springfield: Illinois Centennial Commission, 1920.
Brackenridge, Henry Marie. *Recollections of the Persons
  and Places in the West.* Philadelphia: J. B. Lippin-
  cott, 1966.
Brown, Joseph C. U.S. Survey of Ste. Genevieve.
  1842.
Caldwell, Dorothy J., ed. *Catalog Missouri Historical
  Sites.* Columbia: State Historical Society of
  Missouri, 1963.
Caldwell, Norman Ward. *The French in the Mississippi
  Valley.* Urbana: University of Illinois Press, 1941.
Caruso, John Anthony. *The Mississippi Valley
  Frontier.* Indianapolis: Bobbs-Merrill, 1966.
Chapman, Carl H. *The Missouri Archaeologist.*
  (October 1946).
Chapman, Carl H. and Eleanor F. *Indians and
  Archaeology of Missouri.* Columbia: University of
  Missouri Press, 1964.

Childs, Marquis W. "Two centuries look down upon this home; Valle House, Ste. Genevieve, Mo." *Better Homes and Gardens.* March 1934, 34-54.

Collot, George H. V. *A Journey in North America.* Paris: Arthur Bertrand, Bookseller, 1826.

Dorrance, Ward Allison. *The Survival of French in the Old District of Sainte Genevieve.* Columbia: University of Missouri Press, 1935.

Drury, John. *Historic Midwest Houses.* Minneapolis: University of Minnesota Press, 1947.

"Fort de Chartes State Park." Illinois Department of Conservation, 1964.

"Fort Kaskaskia." Illinois Department of Conservation, 1966.

Franzwa, Gregory M. *The Old Cathedral.* St. Louis: Patrice Press, 1964.

Garcilaso de la Vega. *The Florida of the Inca.* Trans. from the Spanish by John and Jeanette Varner. Austin: University of Texas Press, 1951.

Hinchey, Allan. "El Camino Real," Ste. Genevieve *Herald.* August 17, 1935.

Historic and Beautiful Randolph County. Randolph County Tourism Council, Sparta, Ill.

Houck, Louis. *History of Missouri.* 3 vols. Chicago: R. R. Donnelly and Sons, 1908.

———. *The Spanish Regime.* Chicago: R. R. Donnelly and Sons, 1909.

Hunt, Theodore. *Hunt's Minutes 1825.* Hunt papers, Missouri Historical Society, St. Louis.

Hutchins, Thomas. *A Topical Description of Virginia, Pennsylvania, Maryland and North Carolina, Comprehending the Rivers Ohio, Kenhawa, Sioto, Cherokee, Wabash, Illinois, Mississippi, etc.* London: J. Almon, 1778.

Indian Villages of the Illinois Country. Springfield:
    Illinois State Museum, 1948.

The Jesuit Relations & Allied Documents. 73 vol. ed.
    Reuben Gold Thwaites. Cleveland: Burrows
    1896-1901.

Johnson, Mrs. Charles P. "King of Greece Spent
    Three Months in Ste. Genevieve." Ste. Genevieve
    Fair Play, April 26, 1952.

Kansas City Star. April 25, 1918.

Kellogg, Louise Phelps. *Early Narratives of the
    Northwest, 1634-1699.* New York: C. Scribner's
    Sons, 1917.

Kirschten, Ernest. *Catfish and Crystal.* Garden City,
    New York: Doubleday, 1960.

Laut, Agnes. *Cadillac.* Indianapolis: Bobbs-Merrill,
    1931.

Lightfoot, Zoe Valle. "The Tale of Ste. Genevieve."
    (undated).

Master Plan for Restoration of Ste. Genevieve, Missouri.
    Economic Development Administration, U.S.
    Department of Commerce. Allied Engineers and
    Architects, Inc. St. Louis, 1966.

McDermott, John Francis, ed. *The French in the
    Mississippi Valley.* Urbana: University of Illinois
    Press, 1965.

Missouri, A Guide to the "Show Me" State. WPA
    Writers Program. New York: Duell, Sloan, &
    Pearce, 1941.

Missouri Advocate. St. Louis, May 6, 1825.

Missouri Archaeologist. December 1964.

Missouri Republican. May 8, 1833; April 18, 1815;
    May 2, 1825.

"Missouri's Oldest Settlement," Ste. Genevieve:
    Ste. Genevieve Chamber of Commerce, 1935.

Palm, Mary Borgias. "The Jesuit Missions of the Illinois Country, 1673-1763." Ph.D. diss., St. Louis University, 1931.

Peterson, Charles E. "Colonial St. Louis, Building a Creole Capital." *Bulletin of the Missouri Historical Society* (1947).

Peterson, Charles E. "A Guide to Ste. Genevieve, With Notes on its Architecture." National Park Service, 1939.

Petrequin, Harry J. *Stories of Old Ste. Genevieve,* 1934.

Pittman, Philip. *The Present Site of the European Settlements on the Mississippi.* Cleveland, 1906 (1767).

Reyling, August. O.F.M. *Historical Kaskaskia,* St. Louis, 1963.

Rothensteiner, John. *History of the Archdiocese of St. Louis.* St. Louis, 1928.

Rozier, Firman A. *Rozier's History of the Early Settlement of the Mississippi Valley.* St. Louis: G. A. Pierrot and Son, 1890.

Ste. Genevieve *Fair Play.* Bicentennial Edition, August 17, 1935.

Ste. Genevieve *Herald.* Bicentennial Edition, August 17, 1935.

St. Louis Post-Dispatch. August 31, 1924.

Schaaf, Ida M. "The Founding of Ste. Genevieve, Missouri." *The Missouri Historical Review* 22 (1933): 145-50.

Schlarman, Joseph. *From Quebec to New Orleans; The Story of the French in America.* Belleville, Ill.: Buechler, 1929.

Schoolcraft, Henry Rowe. *Lead Mines of Missouri.* New York: Chas. Wiley, 1819.

Schultz, Christian. *Travels on an Inland Voyage.* New York, 1807-08.

Southeast Missourian. April 28, 1925.

Stoddard, Amos. *Sketches, Historical and Descriptive of Louisiana.* Philadelphia: Mathew Carey, 1812.

Study, Guy, and Voelker, F. E. "Old Settlement Country," 1951.

Temple, Wayne C. *Indian Villages of the Illinois Country — Historic Tribes.* Springfield, Ill., 1958.

Thwaites, Reuben Gold, ed., *Early Western Travels.* Cleveland: Arthur H. Clark, 1904-07.

Twain, Mark. *Life on the Mississippi.* Boston: James R. Osgood, 1883.

Woman's Club of Ste. Genevieve. "Historical Highlights of Ste. Genevieve," 1963.

Yealy, Francis J., S. J. *Sainte Genevieve, The Story of Missouri's Oldest Settlement.* Ste. Genevieve: Bicentennial Historical Committee, 1935.

Personal Communication

Balser, Leo., 1967.

Bannon, John Francis, S. J., 1967.

Blake, Leonard W., 1966.

Brown, Leroy R., 1965.

Cassoutt, Charles., 1967.

Connally, Ernest Allen. "Restoration of the Bolduc House" (ms. in author's possession); letter to author, 1967.

Donze, Mr. and Mrs. Norbert H., 1965, 1966, 1967.

Ellaby, Charles H., Jr., 1965, 1966, 1967.

Foley, Mrs. G. Frederic, 1966.

Hiller, Lena Boyer, 1967.

Lanning, Glennon, 1965.

Lanning, Mrs. R. C., 1967.

Okenfuss, Vera, 1965, 1966, 1967.

Porterfield, Neil, 1965, 1966, 1967.

Ribault, Alonzo, 1966.

Rozier, Mrs. Henry L., 1965, 1966.

Schaffer, E. J., 1966.

Schram, Mr. and Mrs. Bernard K., 1966, 1967.

Sexauer, Mr. and Mrs. Raymond, 1966, 1967.

Vallé, Mrs. Jules, 1965, 1967.

Way, Frederick, Jr., 1967.

Wenzlick, Roy, 1965.

Wolf, Joseph, 1967.

Ziegler, Matthew E., 1965, 1966, 1967.

Index

Credits

Photography:
    By the author, unless otherwise indicated.
Camera:
    Kalimar Six-Sixty, Kaligar 1:2.8, 80mm lens
      (Stanley Photo Company, St. Louis)
Photographic Printing:
    L. Allen Klope, Alton, Illinois.

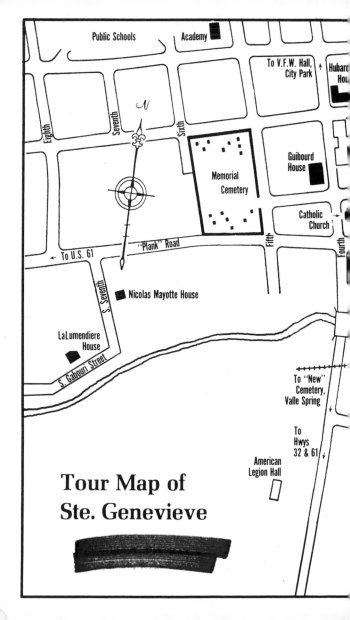

Tour Map of Ste. Genevieve